Goldilocks and Three Bears

A Pantomime

John Morley

Samuel French - London
New York - Toronto - Hollywood

Please see page iv for further copyright information.

CHARACTERS

Sadie Spangle, the owner of the Circus
Goldilocks, her daughter, the animal helper
Ronnie the Ringmaster, her friend
Joey Wizzbang, the Clown
Belinda, the bareback rider
Father Bear
Mother Bear
Baby Bear
Benjamin Black, the owner of the Black Circus*
Pedro Twoface, the gypsy, his evil crony

Performers at Sadie Spangle's Circus, Guardians of the Magic Pool, Gypsies, Black Guards at the Black Circus

If you wish to personalize some of the chorus parts— and it is more fun for the artistes to do this—then in all the Circus Scenes the following can appear in appropriate costumes and are thus "small parts" rather than "chorus".

Iva Sayftinette, the female trapeze artist
Tryan Liftit, the strong man
Fiona Phang, the snake woman
Two Hussars, Lady Acrobats par excellence
Oregon Trayle, the Cowboy ropethrower
Flora Flingmeup, the Juggler
Willy Widemouth, the sword swallower
Mimi Mussentslip, the lady tightrope walker
Stanley Stiletto, the knife thrower
Drum Majorettes

*AUTHOR'S NOTE

Should the name "Benjamin Black" cause any offence it can be changed to a name that "scans" the same, e.g. "Gentleman Jack".   J.M.

ACT I

ACT II

The synopsis of scenes above may appear complicated, but it is not: see Scenery Notes

AUTHOR'S NOTE

This *Goldilocks* pantomime is adapted from the one about which the *Guardian* said "This script has everything. It is People's Pantomime" and if the story is played sincerely—as though it really is happening—I think you, and your audience, will enjoy it.

J.M.

CHARACTER DESCRIPTIONS

Sadie Spangle—is just as her name implies. She is a gutsy circus woman with a heart of gold. Her clothes are gaudy, glittery, and perhaps she has a carrot red wig.

Goldilocks—She is not the Cinderella type, she is Sadie's daughter so is a Circus type with guts. She is pretty but determined, and a tomboy. She must, of course, have blonde hair.

Ronnie The Ringmaster—He may be good at putting on the Circus Ringmaster's voice for announcements, but he is a kind-hearted soul, looking for love: the principal boy, preferably female, in a bright red ringmaster's tail coat and glossy top hat.

Joey Wizzbang—is a crazy clown in clown costume and possibly with clown make-up. The part can be played by an extrovert male or female!

Benjamin Black (Bloodthirsty Black) is an out-and-out villain, wears a black tail coat and top hat and carries a whip.

Belinda—is the bareback rider and she must wear the same type clothes as a traditional pantomime fairy, which bareback riders do anyway. She need not be young and she is not efficient sometimes, but she *is* most anxious to help, and is a bit eccentric.

Father Bear, Mother Bear, Baby Bear—may all be played by females and may all wear the same style of animal skins but **Father** is clearly the proud husband and father, a bit pompous. **Mother** is concerned for him, and trying to discipline Baby Bear who is full of mischief. They have quite separate "walks", and "mime". **Father** can wear a Sherlock Holmes hat, **Mother** a lady's hat, and **Baby** a baseball cap in some scenes. Similarly, their dances are in character with their personalities. It is best to speak the voices into an offstage microphone (there is not much dialogue) as the masks are best covering all the head, consequently, the voices cannot be heard due to these masks. If preferred, their faces *can* show but the first idea is better, especially as the audience wants the famous bears to look as they do in a story book.

Pedro Twoface—is as his name implies. He is only in Act II but at first seems to be friendly and helpful, and then we see he is as wicked as Mr Black.

The rest of the cast are needed for **Guardians of the Magic Pool,** and **Gypsies** and **Black Guards.** But as already mentioned, in the circus scenes they are small parts and can have some fun ideas—it is all according to the size of the cast. Their costumes and characters seem quite clear and they can be mostly played as *female parts.*

PRODUCTION NOTES

The very large, three-foot-long handkerchief which **Joey** produces (Act I, Scene 1) should be threaded through a hole in his trouser pocket, so that it hangs down inside the baggy trousers.

The "Twelve Days of Christmas" television routine can, if desired, be done with a smaller cut-out set to stand in front of each person—thus there would be five sets instead of one. Either way is workable, depending on the size of the stage, and the way in which the comedy business is worked out.

Act I, Scene 5: **Belinda** brings the cottage to life by "magic". This can be done in a half-light, various people—with stylized movements—opening up the front of the cottage and moving the furniture into position downstage. The cottage could, if necessary, have no door, **Goldilocks** simply miming opening it.

Act II, Scene 1: the "Tree of Truth" routine. For this a bench or log is required, and directly above it, foliage to mask a simple grid or trough with two accurate places where the "apples" can fall from above on to areas (1) and (2)—that is, where **Sadie** and **Pedro** sit below. Another method is for the first two "apples" to be fastened to nylon lines, which are released to ensure the "apples" land exactly on **Pedro's** or **Sadie's** head. They can then be pulled up again. However, by far the simplest way to work this routine is to have a stage hand up a step-ladder that is masked by a caravan or the trunk of a tree, and the stage hand can throw the "apples" down on to **Pedro** or **Sadie**. The climax of the routine is *many* "apples" falling at once, and more than one stage hand would be required for this. The "apples" can be fairly large rubber balls, but not the shiny painted type, as balls that bounce too much are not satisfactory.

Act II, Scene 4: it is perfectly in order, if **Joey** finds all the cues in the "Girl Guide" sequence hard to remember, for him to have them written out on his clip board, and deliberately refer to it when giving all the various commands.

Act II, Scene 5: a neat variation on the **Sadie/Gorilla** routine: **Sadie** takes a hand-mirror from her handbag and gives it to the **Gorilla,** who gazes at itself, then peers closely into the mirror, then straightens its hair and preens itself. Finally, still admiring itself, the **Gorilla** exits, elegantly parading off to suitable music.

The most suitable period for costumes, scenery and melodramatic scenes is the Victorian. If a complete break with tradition is desired they can, of course, be played in modern style—but the Victorian does seem to give the most satisfactory results.

SCENERY NOTES

As already stated, the list of scenes seems complicated but is not. For instance, we return several times to the **Circus Ring Scene.**

This **Circus** subject can be presented with just small cut-out pieces, as you will realize from the script. This method is attractive for a small stage. The following few scenery notes are for a normal-sized production.

In Act I, **The Interior of Sadie's Tent** and **The Bears' Cottage** should be attractive but not constructed in an involved way. Then there are no problems, as all the other scenes are simple to construct.

In Act I, scenes 2, 4, 6 and 8 can be **Tabs** or **Frontcloths.**

Scene 3(A) In The Circus Ring and **Scene 3(B) In Sadie's Tent.** This Scene 3(A) is in fact an empty stage for the main comedy routine of Act I. It ends with the cast singing, and as they sing they move downstage, tabs close behind them and Scene 3(B) can now easily be set up as it is an insert scene consisting of the impression of a small circus tent interior, a practical but small scale bed, and two tables.

The bed may be found cumbersome, occupying wing space before this scene, and it could be merely a mattress on the floor, with cover over. As **Sadie** is a circus person with no money, this is in character. Also for this reason, crates could replace the tables and chair; or use the circus "tubs" used in other scenes.

Scene 5: The Three Bears' Cottage. If this is built on a truck it occupies a lot of space. So, if possible, make it a backcloth with furniture in front (for example, the three little beds can have bed heads painted on the cloth). Or let two walls open up, like doors, to show the COTTAGE INTERIOR. This can be done in a stylized way to music in full view of the audience, if you wish, and stylized stage hands can open it up. The main point is to make this scene really attractive, yet not so complicated that we need a long front-cloth before it. The story has good *pace* and it would be wrong to destroy this pace because of scenery.

It is best to plan all Act I scenery around this cottage moment, remembering the Bears' practical furniture.

ACT II

Scenes 2, 4 and 6 can be tabs or frontcloths. The full-stage scenes in Act II are straightforward; please see their descriptions in the script.

If cut-outs, flats and cloths are used and most trucks and rostras are avoided, there is no difficulty. There is so much action that stylized and impressionist scenery is possible. This particularly applies to the furniture used in **Sadie's Tent** and at **The Three Bears' Cottage,** which need not be real life size furniture—the Bears' beds need only be 3 foot long, for example, if viewed by the audience from the foot to the head.

ACT I

SCENE 1

SADIE SPANGLE'S CIRCUS ARRIVES

The circus-style Overture ends and the CURTAIN *rises*

Trees for wings and open countryside at back or a plain cyclorama. At the upstage corner is part of a big circus tent with flags, ropes, etc. The main part of it is offstage. In other words, the circus tent has been erected on the edge of a wood

Joey, the Clown, runs on, jumps up and down several times, claps his white gloved hands and shouts excitedly over the music

Joey Listen, everybody!
Listen to the sound!
Sadie Spangle's Circus
Has reached the circus ground!
They're pegging down the ropes,
And they're banging with the hammer!
Now the tent is going up!
Now you see the banner!
Acrobats and Jugglers
Tight rope walkers—Clowns!
YES, SADIE SPANGLE'S CIRCUS
HAS COME TO TOWN!

"The March of the Gladiators" is played double forte

In the auditorium almost the entire cast enter noisily as members of the circus, each in character and calling out their respective shouts

All Allez ooop! Here we are again! Wheeee! Roll up, roll up! Is everybody happy? Hullo, hullo, hullo! It's cheap at the price, I say it's cheap at the price! We are the champions! The greatest show on earth! Try your luck, lady, try your luck! All the fun of the fair! In for a penny in for a pound! Bang, crash, wallop! It's a laugh a minute! The time of your life! Whizz bang, whizz bang! Come one, come all! Before your very eyes!

They all reach the stage, shouting to the audience and line the footlights and yell the opening number

SONG 1

After the song, all except Joey exit, waving to the audience

Joey (*calling to the audience*) How's yer father! I said, How's yer father!
(*Comically depressed*) Oh blimey, we've got a right lot here. This is a
Circus! A *Circus*! S-I-R-K-U-Z, Circus! And I'm Joey Wizzbang, the
clown! So when I shout "How's yer father", you shout back "All right".
Let's have a bash then. (*Calling*) How's yer father?

Audience All right.

Joey Oh dear me, no, no, no, no. Not—(*sweet and coy*)—"all right"—but
make it loud and dead common, you know: "*ALL RIGHT!*" So, HOW'S
YER FATHER? (*He jumps about in a frenzy to persuade his friends to
shout back*)

Audience All right!

Joey Still not common enough. Once again—(*hysterically*)—HOW'S YER
FATHER?

Audience All right!

Joey (*with relaxed smile*) Lovely. Common as muck. Beautiful! Yes,
you've really cheered me up! YAROO! (*He jumps in the air and clicks his
feet together*) And I need cheering up, believe me! You saw me and my
friends at the circus, all shouting and yelling. But all that noise is *bluff*.
The truth is, this is Sadie Spangle's Circus all right, but Sadie Spangle's
Circus is a failure. Yes, we've got acrobats and tight rope walkers and
everything but—(*he starts to cry and pulls a comical face*)—the truth is
we're a Flippin' Flop! (*In tears*) Yes—excuse me, I'll get out me hanka-
masqueak.

*He takes out a huge, three-foot-long bright coloured "handkerchief" and he
blows his nose. We hear a raspberry/trombone effect. He then holds open the
vast handkerchief and there is a hole in it*

Yes, some people earn a hundred pounds a week—but me, I earn a
hundred p.! (*He takes a tin of vegetables from other pocket of his baggy
trousers*) That's all there is in a tin of Batchelor's—a hundred pea! And
as for the Human Canon Ball, well he lost his job completely. He got
fired. (*Nostalgically*) And I remember we had two performing dogs and
they were fantastic. One was called Orpheus 'cos he didn't offenbach
and the other was called Sandwich 'cos he was half bred. They were
what's known as miniature poodles—the miniature back was turned
they did a poodle. (*He starts to laugh in a "Goofy" way*) Ha ha ha ha!

Some of the circus folk enter from various places

Acrobat Goldilocks is coming!

All Hullo Goldie! How's life? 'Morning!

Goldilocks enters in circus costume, waving to them all

Joey (*in a clown-style delivery*) Good morning, Goldilocks!

*He backs to the edge of the stage, or towards one of the performers, and thus
collects, unseen, a big prop clownish flower and bowing, takes it from behind
his back and gives it to Goldilocks*

Goldie (*laughing as she collects the big stupid daisy*) Oh! (*Depressed*) Oh
    but Joey, even you can't make me laugh today.
Joey (*making a mad gesture with his hands, then taking off his hat*) Why not?
Goldie Our Circus is doing so badly and it worries me.

Joey claps his hands Eddie Cantor style

Joey But your mother owns the Circus, not you!
Goldie It worries her as well. It's a nice little circus.

All nod heads, agreeing

All Yes!
Goldie But nobody comes to see it.

Joey and others shake heads several times

All No . . .
Goldie The Circus Tent was only half full last night.
All Yes.

Joey nods frantically

Goldie If only we had some fabulous *animal* act!
All Yes!

Joey nods, jumping up and down in the air with enthusiasm at this idea

Goldie *That's* what audiences like, an animal act.

Joey nods

    Oh dear, oh dear . . .

*Joey takes out an unrolling "blower" and blows it out at her face and it
squeaks*

Joey How's yer father?
Goldie (*sadly*) All right . . .
Joe (*to the others*) That won't do, will it?
All No!
Joey How's yer father?
Goldie (*brightening up, calling loudly*) ALL RIGHT! Oh you're right
    Joey! I *must* cheer up! Worry gets you nowhere!
Joey That's right!

          SONG 2 (Short, hectic, bouncy production number)

At the end of the song, all exit except Goldilocks

Goldie (*as she watches them exit*) I love circus folk. (*To the audience*) But
    best of all I love animals. We've only got a few dogs and horses. I wish
    we'd got an elephant or a tiger—or a few bears would be nice! (*She
    looks off*) Oh here's Ronnie.

Ronnie the Ringmaster enters

Ronnie (*singing cornily*) "Hullo Goldie, hullo—bom!" (*He takes off his top hat and bows*) What's all that you were saying about a helephant?
Goldie (*in an outburst*) Oh I'm so unhappy!

Goldilocks runs off

Ronnie Is it something I said? What was all that about, then? (*To the audience*) Is it all the worry about the circus not doing well?
Audience Yes.
Ronnie Poor Goldilocks and poor Sadie Spangle—she owns the circus you know. I'm just the ringmaster. Oh but I haven't introduced myself. That was Goldilocks in charge of the animals and this here is Ronnie the Ringmaster! (*He bows*) I'm in love with Goldie. The circus isn't doing too well and neither am I. She doesn't love me. No.
Audience Aaaaah!
Ronnie Thank you for your sympathy. (*With a huge sigh*) Ho hum—ah me —still, you can't be depressed in a circus can you? You can't be all droopy drawers, not with all the spangles and the music!

SONG 3

Soon the Juveniles enter, miming instrument playing. Then all the circus folk, plus Joey, perhaps, enter for the Production Number

After the number, the circus folk start bringing on brightly coloured parcels and putting them in a pile against the wings

Joey Ronnie, what are we going to do about the circus?
Ronnie Don't ask me, ask Sadie! She owns it! It's a real shame . . .
Joey I don't like to talk about it on her birthday.
Ronnie I'd better go and get her presents!
Joey And I'd better go and wish her many happies. (*He calls*) Where are you, Sadie?
Ronnie (*calling*) Many happy returns and where are you?

Ronnie and Joey exit

First Circus Performer Let's get Sadie's presents!
All Yes let's!
Second Performer She'll be coming from her tent. So put her presents there.

She points to the R wing and Sadie's entrance music starts, and they all put the bright coloured boxes in a small pile by the R wings and then look off L

Third Performer It'll be a surprise for her!

All line up for Sadie's arrival. The pile of presents is sent flying because Sadie enters R. She is clearly the ebullient and gaudily dressed circus owner

Sadie Hullo! Hullo, everybody! Yes it's me, Sadie Spangle, owner of

Sadie Spangle's Spectacular Circus! (*She looks on the floor at the presents*) But what's all this? What is it?

All turn to greet Sadie as she speaks

All Happy birthday, Sadie! Happy birthday, Mrs Spangle!
Sadie Good heavens. I didn't know it was my twenty-third birthday!
A Child It isn't!
Sadie Cheeky devil!

Ronnie enters with a parcel, kisses her and gives her the present

Ronnie Many happy returns.
Sadie Oh thank you, dear! (*Opening the lid of the small box*) What ever is it? (*Overcome*) Oh, Ronnie—oh you shouldn't—oh you can't possibly afford it—oh, Ronnie, I'm overwhelmed by such extravagance. (*She holds it up to the audience*) Look, everybody—a pound of coffee!
Ronnie I knew you'd like it!
Sadie Well everyone, thank you, and will you go and put the presents in my tent—I'll open them later.
All 'Bye, Sadie!

All exit, except Sadie, taking the parcels with them

Sadie Aren't they nice to give me all those lovely pressies! But circus people are like that, and I've been in that world all my life. First I joined a flea circus—yes, I started from scratch. I used to like the fleas—they were always itching to please. (*She scratches herself*) They still are! Mind you, I've got nothing left now but an old bed. Still, it's something to retire on. And life's full of ups and downs. I was a lift attendant at Bertram Mills for a time. But I think the worst thing was when I had the row with the elephant. He was *impossible*. So obstinate, I just had to tell him to pack his trunk and get out. Oh but I love the Circus! I remember I once tried to make a jaguar jump through a hoop—it was nearly the death of me. The wheels got caught in the hoop. Of course it was a *leopard* that made me a widow. He ate my husband. My Fred was a dear, but he was a little man, very little. He was wearing a yellow circus costume at the time and the leopard thought he was a fish finger. But I tell you what I *do* really like—Penguins. (*Opening her big, jazzy handbag*) In fact I've got some on me now! (*She takes a chocolate biscuit out*) Anyone like a Penguin?
Audience Yes!
Sadie I can't hear you. I said "Anyone like a Penguin?"
Audience Yes!
Sadie Here you are then! (*She throws a few out to the audience with various remarks*)
Oh I am sorry, madam! How unfortunate! (*To the rest of the audience*) It's bounced into her bosom! Oh I've forgotten you lot at the back! I used to bowl for—(*she mentions a local cricket team*)—so here it comes! (*She moves upstage, prepares herself by hitching up her skirt, then runs downstage and bowls a Penguin into the back of the stalls. Laughing*) Oh

dear! We do some silly things in the Circus, don't we! Well, it makes you feel good!

SONG 4

All the Circus people enter and sing with her. Two of the men lift her horizontally and take her off for the exit. All now exit

At the same time, Ronnie enters one side holding a newspaper and Goldie enters from the other

Ronnie Feeling better now?

Goldie (*shaking her head*) Not really, no.

Ronnie This might cheer you up. It's in the (local newspaper). It's about a circus performer.

Goldie Well read on—but we can't afford him whoever he is.

Ronnie (*reads out from newspaper*) "The best circus act we have ever seen was called the Irish Father Christmas."

Goldie The *Irish* Father Christmas?

Ronnie (*reading*) "He used to come into the ring on a sledge driven by reindeers, with a big white beard—and a sack full of Easter eggs."

Goldie (*laughing*) Ronnie! Everything's going wrong for us but you always make me laugh!

Ronnie (*with great sincerity*) I'm glad. I'd do anything for you Goldilocks, you know that. Oh, there's something else in the paper—your horoscope.

Goldie I always read that—what does it say?

Ronnie It says . . . (*Reading*) "Aries. Your lucky colour is bright red" (*or whatever is the colour of his flashy coat*) "This week you are going to meet your future husband."

Goldie (*excited*) I am?

Ronnie "And his name begins with an 'R'."

Goldie Begins with an "R" . . . let me think. . . . (*Realizes*) Hey, let me have a look! (*Reading over his shoulder*) "Aries—your lucky colour is dark brown. This week beware of a serious financial problem." It says nothing about my future husband! (*Chiding him*) Ronnie. . . .

Ronnie Well it's a good way of getting you to listen to me!

He sings a NUMBER *and it soon becomes a* DUET

SONG 5

Goldie (*after the song*) I must go and see how Mum's getting on. She's having a super birthday!

Ronnie She's not you know.

Goldie What d'you mean?

Ronnie That horrible man has been to see her again.

Goldie (*gasping*) Benjamin Black? (*She groans*) Oh *no*. . . .

Ronnie Oh yes! He wants to buy the Circus all right. This time it's for real!

Goldie (*worried*) Benjamin Black. Some people are cruel to humans, but he's cruel to *animals*—and animals can't answer back! (*Vehemently*) I think circuses that are cruel to animals should be *stopped by law*. Don't you agree?

Ronnie Yes. Benjamin Black is dead cruel, a real baddie is Benjamin Black.

Goldie Oh. If only there was somebody to save us from him! If Mother sells him the circus, *she'll have to sell the animals.*

Ronnie And Bloodthirsty Black will get them! If only there *was* somebody that could help!

A few bars of strange music are heard

> *Belinda the bareback rider enters. She pauses, not seeing them, tidies her costume, does a "barre" exercise as though in ballet, and wobbles a bit*

Belinda Whoops.

Goldie (*whispering*) There's the new bareback rider, Ronnie. Have you noticed how *mysterious* she is?

Ronnie Yes isn't she? Where did she come from?

Goldie Nobody knows—she just suddenly appeared as if by magic!

Ronnie "Suddenly appeared"? Anyone'd think she was a fairy!

Goldie Ronnie, she looks like one in those clothes.

Ronnie (*laughing*) Don't be daft! That's her circus costume!

Goldie (*calling to Belinda*) Welcome to my mother's Circus! How are you settling in?

Belinda (*jovially*) Fine thanks! I've got a super caravan! It's got a shower in it—and a loo! It's awfully clever how they arrange these things nowadays, isn't it?

Ronnie (*aside to Goldilocks*) Did we say she was a fairy? You're joking of course!

Goldie Ssssh. (*Politely to Belinda*) It's very *nice* to see you, but we can't understand why you've come to such a small circus as ours!

A few bars of strange music are heard as she speaks

Belinda It isn't the size of the place I mind
It's whether the people are good and kind.
If people are wanting you as their friend
Good luck will come to them in the end.

Ronnie (*surprised*) What a nice bit of poetry!

Belinda starts to exit

Oh don't go!

Goldie Anything either of us can do for you?

Belinda You're very kind but I've not finished unpacking yet! The caravan's so small, I can't find anywhere to put my smalls!

Belinda laughs jovially and exits

Ronnie Funny lady! "If people are wanting you as their friend, good luck will come to them in the end . . ."

Goldie Well, we need good luck all right—the circus is almost broke! Mum is getting desperate! Oh Ronnie, if only we had some fabulous trapeze artistes or best of all, a really good animal act like lions or tigers or . . .

Ronnie Or bears!

Goldie *Performing bears!* Oh Ronnie that would pack 'em in wouldn't it! Oh, but Mum could never afford to buy an act like that, we're so poor.

Ronnie (*with gloomy head shaking*) It's a problem without solution . . .

Sadie enters in another gaudy "circusy" type of costume

Sadie Kids, I've got a great new idea for the Circus!

Goldie (*groaning*) Oh not another . . .

Sadie Yes, another! (*With comedy anger*) And don't you speak to your mother like that! I'll show you I'm not a has-been! I've got sawdust running through my veins, I have!

Ronnie (*separating Sadie from Goldie*) Sadie! Mrs Spangle!

Sadie (*not apologizing, pacing to and fro*) We need a new idea and I've *got* a new idea! It's Christmas time isn't it?

Ronnie⎫
Goldie⎭ (*dubiously*) Yes . . . ⎬(*Speaking together*)

Sadie Well this is about Christmas! Let's rehearse it now!

Ronnie⎫
Goldie⎭ (*dubiously*) Well . . . ⎬(*Speaking together*)

Sadie See how it goes!

Ronnie⎫
Goldie⎭ Er . . . ⎬(*Speaking together*)

Sadie Give it a whirl! (*Calling*) Joey, Willy, Prunella, Mimi!

Joey and a few of the Circus folk enter

Joey (*to the audience*) How's yer father?

Audience All right!

Joey (*giving the thumbs-up sign*) Lovely!

Sadie becomes all chaotic bustle, going to and fro, "organizing"

Sadie Kids, I've got a great new idea for the circus! (*Triumphantly*) It's a roundelay!

Joey A roundy what?

Sadie (*pointing off*) Bring those things here, will you?

A few of the circus folk exit and return with a big television set cut-out and all the props required. The front of the cut-out is made like a big television set with open panel so that when standing up behind it, the person's head and shoulders are clearly seen. This open "screen" is perhaps three foot by four foot, and below it are the typical television knobs painted on. Hinged sides represent this over-large television set

(*Meanwhile*) It's simple! I'll teach it you in a minute. It'll bring the tent down!

Ronnie I hope it doesn't!

Sadie You just sing "The first thing this Christmas I noticed on TV" and then *keep everything under control*—right?

Ronnie, Joey and a few others agree optimistically and then join Sadie in singing

They all stand each side of the television screen and rush into the screen and pop up there with the various articles as they are mentioned in the lyric. Sadie in particular is soon in complete shambles, with Joey not much better

SONG 6

(*Singing*) The first thing this Christmas I noticed on TV was a bottle containing Squeegee.

She holds up bottle, squirts liquid out at the audience. It may well hit the front rows but it is in fact water

Ronnie The second thing this Christmas I noticed on TV
was two kinky boots (*He holds them up*)
Sadie And a bottle containing Squeegee. (*She squirts it*)
Joey The third thing this morning I noticed on TV
was three tins of fruits. (*He holds them up, drops one*)
Ronnie Two kinky boots. (*He holds them up*)
Sadie And a bottle containing Squeegee. (*She squirts it*)
Juggler On the fourth day of Christmas I noticed on TV
four Porridge Oats. (*He holds up the packet into the prop TV set, drops one, shambles*)
Joey Three tins of fruits.
Ronnie Two kinky boots. (*He holds them up into the TV set*)
Sadie And a bottle containing Squeegee. (*She squirts it*)
Acrobat On the fifth day of Christmas I noticed on TV
Five Cross-Your-Heart bras! (*He picks them up and waves them out of TV set*)
Juggler Four Porridge Oats.
Joey Three tins of fruits.
Ronnie Two kinky boots.
Sadie And a bottle containing Squeegee.

The routine repeats itself, but faster

On the sixth day of Christmas I noticed on TV
Six fishy fingers. (*A packet shaped like six fingers*)
Acrobat Five Cross-Your-Heart bras.
Juggler Four Porridge Oats.
Joey Three tins of fruits.
Ronnie Two kinky boots.
Sadie And a bottle containing Squeegee.

We are now half-way through the number and other prop suggestions are hair lotion, Gorgonzola cheese, soaps for shaving, curley wurley sweets, non-stick pans, mince marvels, and "Nine Nasty Nappies" is a good line. There are also cornflake packets, scotch whisky, grounded grains

The routine ends with all singing full blast "And a bottle containing Squeegee" and with most of them in complete chaos, especially Sadie

Black-out

SCENE 2

THE WOODS NEAR THE CIRCUS

Tabs or frontcloth of woods, and perhaps the circus tent can be seen through the trees

Dramatic music, dim lighting, green spotlight, as Benjamin Black enters looking around him. He is in top hat and black tails and riding breeches and boots. He carries a bull whip

Black So! (*Cracking his whip*) My name is Benjamin Black, known to most people—and that includes *you*—as Bloodthirsty Black! Ha ha ha! I own the biggest Circus in the world! And do you know why I own the biggest Circus in the world? I BUY UP ALL THE LITTLE CIRCUSES! Circuses like this one of Sadie Spangle's. Ha ha ha! Once I've got a circus in my power then I turn on the animals and I "train" them—with this! (*He cracks his whip*) Ha ha ha ha!

Music starts

No wonder they call me Bloodthirsty Black! And being cruel has made me so *rich*! (*He sings gleefully*)

SONG 7

(*After the song*) Once I've got Sadie Spangle's Circus in my power then I'll train her little dogs and ponies *my* way . . . (*He cracks his whip*) Ha ha ha! (*With heavy sarcasm*) Poor little things! (*He cracks his whip*) Ha ha ha!

During the above the audience start booing; he runs down a couple of the steps to the audience and threatens them

Don't you boo me! Because I'm not a fool am I?
Audience Yes.
Black Silence, you pathetic peasants! Oh, so we're *booing* Bloodthirsty Black are we? Listen, you crummy collection of insignificant idiots, if I get down amongst you lot, I'll have a whip round! (*He sees someone off*) Ah, here comes Sadie Spangle, I must compose myself. (*He stands in a haughty and dignified pose*)

Sadie enters

Sadie Hullo, Fatty!
Black How dare you!
Sadie What are you doing here, snooping round in the woods near my Circus?
Black I've come to see you and you're looking very attractive, Sadie . . .
Sadie (*flattered*) Oh! Thank you! (*Aside to the audience*) He wants something. And I'll tell you something else. He's not going to get it.
Black It's not your Circus, it's *you* that I want.

Sadie Liar. You *do* want to buy the Circus from me, don't you?

Black Yes I do, you obstinate old frump! I'll give you good money for your Circus!

Sadie I'm not selling!

Black When I say good money I mean good money.

Sadie I'm not selling!

Black When I say good money I mean *fifty thousand pounds.*

Sadie I'm not sell . . . (*unable to believe it*) Fifty thousand pounds????
(*Recovers*) Oh I know you of old, Benjamin Black. If I sold my circus to you, you'd be cruel and horrible. You'd *hurt* my lovely monkeys and parrots and horses and—

Black Then you're not selling?

Sadie Certainly not. I haven't a penny but I'M NOT SELLING MY CIRCUS.

Black (*aside*) I must do this gently. (*To Sadie*) If you haven't a penny, can I lend you three pounds?

Sadie Certainly not. Well—it would buy the monkeys a few nuts. Ta . . .

Black You know me. Always happy to help a friend. (*He gives her the three pounds then feels in his pocket*)

Black Oh one moment, I've just realized I shall need that three pounds myself and *I've lent you all I had.*

Sadie (*magnanimously*) Tell you what, I'll lend you a pound.

Black (*sarcastically*) Oh, thank you!

Sadie Now I owe you two pounds.

Black Yes.

Sadie You owe me one pound.

Black (*after a pause, a bit puzzled*) Er—yes.

Sadie Well here's the two pounds I owe you, you give me the pound you owe me. (*She gives him two pounds, snatches one pound from him and starts to exit*)

Black One moment, Sadie, I don't quite understand how this works out.

Sadie You can't see it?

Black No.

Sadie Well, I tell you what, you pretend to be me and I'll pretend to be you lending me the three pounds.

Black (*very reluctantly*) Right. Sadie, lend me three pounds.

Sadie (*counting out the three*) One—two—three . . . (*She realizes*) Oh dear, I've lent you all I have.

Black Right. I'll lend you a pound. That's what you said wasn't it?

Sadie Yes. Now I owe you a pound.

Black Yes.

Sadie You owe me two pounds.

Black (*after much hesitation*) Er—yes . . .

Sadie (*quickly*) Well, there's the pound I owe you, and you give me the two pounds you owe me. (*She snatches two pounds from him and starts to walk off*)

Black *Just* a minute, Sadie! I don't understand this at all. I started off with three pounds, then I had two pounds—what's the meaning of this? Now I've only one pound.

Sadie You still can't see it?

Black No, I certainly can't.

Sadie (*taking the pound from him*) O.K., Benjamin Black, ask me again!

Black Right. Sadie lend me three pounds.

Sadie One—two—three. (*She counts them out, into his hand*) Now you owe me three pounds.

Black Er—yes . . .?

Sadie Well then, Benjamin—LET'S HAVE 'EM!

Sadie grabs them and runs off

Black That's not right! I've lost out on the deal! Come here!

Loud vaudeville music

Black chases Sadie off

Black-out, followed at once by a spot on the other side of the stage

Belinda enters into the spotlight. She addresses the audience confidentially and intimately

Belinda So that is Mister Benjamin Black!
His schemes I'm going to hinder
Yes somehow I am going to fight back
Or my name's not Belinda.
I'll *pretend* I'm a horseback rider
(I know nothing about these things)
I may look like a bareback rider
But see—big sensation—*WINGS!*

She turns round and shows wings attached at her back—or lifts up her arms and "butterfly wings" are attached to her wrists

These circus folk have cause for alarm
They're right to be so wary
But I'll protect them all from harm
As you see . . . *I'm really a fairy!*

Belinda exits triumphantly, waving her wand

At once we hear Joey's loud and raucous voice on the offstage microphone, or perhaps he puts his head through the centre of the tabs in the traditional clown style

Joey (*off*) Come to the Circus—come to the show!
Over to the Circus ring—let's go!

Loud music and fanfare

SCENE 3(a)

IN THE CIRCUS RING

The front cloth is flown, or Tabs open to reveal the Circus ring

CIRCUS PRODUCTION ROUTINE

This is the main Act I routine and is adaptable. It involves Sadie (who must leave the routine before it ends) Goldilocks, Ronnie, Joey and all the small parts that represent the Circus

*The Pantomime Director will be seeing this routine as an entity in itself, as a way of showing our audience just what Sadie's Circus is like, and it is at Scene 3(b) that we return to plot dialogue. So "*SCENE 3(a) *'In the Circus Ring'* " *is a comedy routine involving most of the cast and it is to be found at* the end of this script *so that it can be treated quite separately*

SCENE 3(a) *ends with everyone moving down stage and singing a song about clowns.* (SONG 8) *After it the tabs close, opening again to reveal Scene 3(b)*

SCENE 3(b)

THE INTERIOR OF SADIE'S TENT. *Night-time, after the show*

This is a simple insert scene with a very small bed, small table piled high with bills, maybe a stool. It could even be a mattress on the floor and some crates, or circus "tubs"

Sadie is sitting at the table

Sadie (*throwing bills over her shoulder*) Gas bill—electric bill—television rental—telephone bill. (*To the audience*) What about the phone bills, aren't they *shocking*? I don't know about you but I can't pay them so that's that! (*She scoops up the whole lot and throws them up in the air*) D'you know something? Me and Goldilocks are so poor we're living off bread and jam! (*She picks up a plastic carrier bag*) She went shopping earlier so I wonder what she bought. (*She looks in the carrier bag; pleased*) Oh I say—instead of bread and jam she's bought bread and honey!

She takes out the wrapped bread and the big prop jar that is clearly labelled "HONEY" and puts them on the table as Goldilocks enters with a few pound notes. She is still in the clown costume and takes off her hat, shakes out her hair, takes off the red nose on elastic.

Goldie Hullo Mum, here are tonight's takings, they're not too bad.

Sadie (*taking the pile of notes; kindly*) Goldie, they're terrible and you know it. (*She sighs*) All the money we've got in the world.

Goldie I'll put them in the safe. (*She stares*) Where's the safe gone?

Sadie I sold it this morning. I had to pay the acrobats.

Goldie Are things as bad as that! (*She looks round*) Then where can we hide the money? What about under the mattress?

Sadie That's the first place anyone would look.

Goldie Well we must find somewhere that'll be safe until morning.

Sadie (*she looks round and is suddenly inspired*) I've got it! I'll put it in the bread! Is it sliced?

Goldie (*laughs*) Yes! But you can't put the money in the bread!

Sadie Why not? No one'll look for it there, now will they? (*Picking up the bread and opening the wrapping*) Oh and thank you for the honey—makes a nice change.

She puts the notes in the bread, closes the wrapping again and puts the bread and the honey jar back in the carrier bag

Goldie Well I know you like honey. (*She checks the carrier bag*) I suppose you're right! No one would ever think of looking for money in some sliced bread! (*She laughs and puts down the carrier near the bed*)

Sadie You are pretty when you laugh. I suppose that's why Ronnie loves you.

Goldie Oh Mum—he loves me and I don't love him!

Sadie That happened to me once. It was years ago now. He was very handsome. He worked at—(*a big local factory, or where a party booking that performance has come from*)—and all the girls were mad about him. He had a face like Paul Newman, Robert Redford and John Revolta rolled into one.

Goldie (*gently*) And you married him . . .

Sadie No. I married your father and he had a face like a stewed prune.

Goldie Oh I'll never marry Ronnie!

Sadie No, dear.

Goldie I mean, he's just a friend!

Sadie Yes, dear.

Goldie So I don't *love* him.

Sadie No, dear.

Goldie But I do *like* him.

Sadie Yes, dear.

Goldie Do *you* like men?

Sadie No, dear—what am I saying. Yes, dear, they're gorgeous.

Goldie Which ones are gorgeous?

Sadie When you're my age, ALL OF 'EM! And now say good night to your old Mum.

Goldie Nightie nightie. (*She kisses her*)

Sadie Pyjama pyjama.

Goldie exits

Ah me, time for bed I suppose . . .

The razzy music starts and Sadie goes into the Strip Routine. It ends with Sadie jumping into the bed, and pulling the cover over her at exactly the same moment as the music ends. She is instantly asleep, maybe we hear a few snores

Belinda enters to strange music

Belinda They think I'm part of the Circus show
Riding round the ring on a horse!
But as I told you long ago
I'm not really that of course!
Although I wear the circus frocks
And through the hoop I leap
I'm really the *Guardian of Goldilocks*
And her mother fast asleep.

To Sadie, who is lying fast asleep

Because you are good and not afraid
I'll summon someone to your aid
Someone to bring you joy and laughter
And soon you'll live happy ever after!

Belinda beckons off with her wand, then exits

Suitable Teddy Bear music is heard

Father Bear pops round the scenery, enters, beckons to offstage and Mother Bear enters. Then she beckons and Baby Bear jumps in. Father and Mother look round in a dignified way but Baby Bear is curious about everything, running round the tent interior

Dramatic chord of music. He stops still and sniffs. Father and Mother Bear also react and then sniff. Baby Bear follows the scent, sniffing around, arms held out almost as though water divining and the scent leads him to the carrier bag which he holds up, opens and sniffs

He beckons to Mother and Father, all look in the plastic bag and nod several times with delight. Baby Bear jumps up and down when Mother holds up the honey jar

At this noise Sadie groans in her sleep and turns over in bed. The Three Bears now notice her, react, and dither about. Then Father Bear grabs the carrier bag from Baby Bear and sternly points offstage and the Three Bears exit fast

Sadie (*groaning then waking and sitting up dramatically*) There's a man in my tent! There's a man in my tent! (*With great disappointment*) No there isn't. I'm dreaming again. Oh well, as long as the money's safe and sound in the carrier bag I can go off to sleep again and—(*She has put her hand out to pat the bag. She gropes round and realizes with horror that it isn't there. Yells*) The money! Thief! Robber! Thug! Bandit! Burglar! Crook! Villain! (*She has jumped quickly from the bed or mattress and in her agony, she moves downstage as she shouts*) Oh my heart! Oh my money! It's gone! (*She starts to sob*) It's the money to pay the circus people! (*Shouts*) Help!

The tabs close behind her as downstage (in front of the tabs) Ronnie, Goldilocks, Joey and various sleepy Circus People enter from each side, rubbing their eyes, only half awake

(*to Joey*) Someone's stolen the carrier bag!

Joey (*blankly, half asleep*) Ay?

Sadie (*to Ronnie*) Someone's stolen the carrier bag!

Ronnie (*also blank*) I don't understand!

Sadie (*to audience*) I'll go mad in a minute. (*To Goldilocks, very loudly*) Someone's stolen the carrier bag!

Goldie (*horrified*) And the money's in the bread!

Sadie Right! (*To all the group*) Everything I possess—all the money that I owe you for salary—I hid it in the carrier bag and the bag's gone!

Everyone reacts

Ronnie It's the gypsies down the road—they've stolen it!

All Yes—the gypsies down the road—it's the gypsies!

Ronnie They're always up to something. I'll go down to the gypsy camp right now! (*He starts to exit*)

Sadie Just a minute.

Ronnie (*turning to her*) What is it?

Sadie (*with much curiosity*) Why would anybody steal a *carrier bag*? They couldn't possibly know I hid the money in the bread. We must *think* . . .

Joey We must use our loaf! (*He laughs "Goofily"*) Ha ha ha—

All Stop!

Joey (*he stops laughing*) Sorry.

Goldie You mean, why would the gypsies bother to steal some bread and honey . . .

Sadie I'm flummoxed. (*To the audience*) Unless—any of you see what happened?

Audience Yes!

Joey Was it the gypsies?

Audience No!

Sadie Then who was it?

Audience Three Bears—the Bears, etc.

Goldie The *what*?

All the Circus troupe line the footlights asking questions

Audience Three Bears!

Sadie, Ronnie, Goldilocks and Joey are amazed

The Four THREE BEARS???

Ronnie Which way did they go?

Sadie (*pointing the wrong way*) This way?

Audience No.

Goldie This way?

Audience Yes!

Ronnie Then after them!

Sadie Come on everybody—come on—(*A rallying call*)—FIND THE THREE BEARS!

Dramatic music, as Sadie strides off, all the others following; all exit on one side

The Lights fade to a Black-out

SCENE 4

THE CHASE THROUGH THE WOODS

The tabs remain closed or we see the SCENE 2 *"Woods" frontcloth, dimly lit*

"Teddy Bear" music at fast tempo, or "Can Can" music, is heard and now the Bears cross. Mother and Father holding the carrier bag, Baby entering late. They are suddenly aware someone is following them, turn round, point to offstage, and panic. They start to run on the spot. Strobe lighting (or just a spotlight) plays on them, C

Shouts are heard off, then Sadie, Ronnie, Joey and Goldie and all the Circus Folk enter, and a comedy chase starts in the flickering light

COMEDY CHASE

During the chase, the Bears exit, put on police helmets, return, and move all the Circus Folk on as though directing traffic

Then, in the flickering light, a Gorilla enters

After a while Sadie suddenly sees it and tries to point it out to her friends. All are still running on the spot. Her friends each pass on the message to each other, each sees the Gorilla in turn and puts up his or her arms in a panic gesture

After the chase, all exit, the Bears have got away in the confusion

The bustle music slows down to mysterious music

Goldilocks enters in front of the tabs, slowly gazing round and scared

Goldie I must be in the middle of the wood that's near the circus . . .

To the mysterious music, the Tabs slowly open or the gauze dissolves, we see Belinda behind the gauze "magicing" the scene change

Belinda Goldilocks, no need for distress
The Three Bears bring you Happiness . . .

The woodcloth gauze is flown, or the tabs open

Belinda points to the upstage cottage and exits, still unseen by Goldilocks

SCENE 5

THE THREE BEARS' COTTAGE IN THE WOODS

Goldilocks looks at the cottage with delight

Goldie Well! What a surprise! A nice little house deep in the woods! There's nobody about—perhaps the person that lives there is inside. I could peep through the windows to find out . . . no, I'll go straight inside! (*She walks upstage*) I'm getting so tired, and I'm sure the owner will give me a bed for the night . . .

However arranged, she "enters" the cottage

(*Looking round*) It's very neat and tidy—obviously it's owned by a lady who is really houseproud! (*She notices the small table*) Oh look, breakfast is ready! Cornflakes! No it's not, it's *porridge*! Three bowls of porridge for three people! I know I shouldn't taste it but I'm so hungry I'm afraid I'm going to! (*Picking up the spoon by the first bowl, she tastes the porridge and shouts*) OW! That's too hot for me . . . (*She tastes the next one with the spoon and pulls a face*) EURCCH! That's too *cold* for me . . . what about this one. (*She tastes the third bowl*) That's neither too hot nor too cold but just right. And I like it so well, I shall eat it all up. Oh I *am* hungry. Nobody's about so I'll forget my table manners . . . (*She gulps down the spoonfulls of porridge in an unladylike way, making a lot of noise, then smacks her lips*) Smashing! (*She notices the chairs*) And look—three chairs! I could do with a nice sit down. (*She sits on the big chair*) Too hard for me . . . (*She sits on the medium chair*) too soft for me . . . (*She sits on the small chair*) This one's neither too hard nor too soft but just right. (*She sighs*) Yes, just right . . .

She leans back contentedly. We hear a loud splintering effect at the offstage microphone or percussion sounds and she starts

Oh! (*She feels the seat of the chair*) Oh dear! (*She stands up and examines it*) I think I've broken the bottom of the chair! And I was hoping to go to sleep! (*She looks round*) I wonder if the lady that owns the place has got any beds? (*Looking round, she sees the bed area*) Ah! (*Sitting on the first small bed*) Too hard! (*Sitting on the second bed*) Too soft! (*Sitting on the third bed*) Neither too hard . . . nor . . . too soft . . . but . . . just . . . right . . . (*She yawns*)

She closes her eyes, leans back and lying on the bed she at once falls asleep

Downstage the Three Bears enter to their music

They go into the house (however it is arranged) and we hear the three distinctly different voices at the offstage microphone as Father Bear wanders over to the table and reacts hugely. They play the scene exactly as it was written in 1837:

Father Bear Somebody's been at my porridge!

Mother Bear (*noticing and equally indignant*) Somebody's been at *my* porridge!

Baby Bear (*even more indignant*) Somebody's been at my porridge and eaten it all up!

All three Bears look around suspiciously and then, as before, Father Bear reacts hugely

Father Bear Somebody's been sitting in my chair!

Mother Bear Somebody's been sitting in *my* chair!

Baby Bear Somebody's been sitting in my chair and has *sat the bottom out of it*!

Father Bear points firmly towards the bed area and they cross to it. Their indignation makes them speak faster now

Father Bear Somebody's been lying in my bed!
Mother Bear Somebody's been lying in *my* bed!
Baby Bear Somebody's been lying in *my* bed—and she still is! (*Shaking Goldilocks*) Naughty! Wake up, you!

Goldilocks wakes up and is frightened out of her wits at seeing three bears hovering over her

Goldie Help! Three bears!
Father Bear (*indignantly*) We're not three bears. We're *THE* three bears. We won't hurt you.
Goldie Thank goodness for that!
Mother Bear But my dear, we do think you've taken a liberty.
Goldie I'm sorry.
Baby Bear A *diabolical* liberty, if you ask me!
Goldie (*hearing his squeaky voice, she is delighted*) A baby bear!
Baby Bear I'm not a baby bear. I shall be eleven next week.
Goldie I apologize. As you'll be eleven next week I'll fake it a few years and I'll call you a *teenage* bear. Would you like that?

Baby Bear nods

Father Bear (*sternly*) Nevertheless, you've stolen our porridge!
Goldie Well you've stolen my money.
The Three Bears What money?
Goldie It's no use playing the innocent with me. You've hidden the carrier bag so that I won't know you've stolen the money, but unfortunately for you I know that you *have* stolen the money.

Mother Bear collects the carrier from somewhere near, holds it up and Goldilocks takes out the bread

Goldie (*sternly*) Now. Where is the— Why, the money's still in the sliced loaf! Then what on earth did you take the carrier bag for?

Baby Bear takes out the jar marked "HONEY" and holds it up, pointing to the label

Oh of *course*! Bears like honey don't they?
The Three Bears Yes! (*They nod several times*)
Goldie I'm terribly sorry. (*Realizing*) You didn't want the money, you wanted the *honey*!

All four laugh. Baby Bear guiltily hands the honey jar to her

Oh I wouldn't *dream* of taking it back! It wouldn't make sense! I mean, nobody could take honey from a bear could they? Besides, it's a rather *good* honey as it happens. (*She hands it back to Baby Bear*)

Baby Bear jumps for joy and is joined by Mother and Father. They are so pleased they go into a mad little quick comedy bit—just a few steps of a comedy routine

> (*Laughing*) Oh that's good! It's like a circus routine and . . . (*It dawns on her*) It's like a circus routine! Oh Bears, Bears, will you do something for me?

They are not sure. But Baby Bear nods many times

> I mean, I know it's nice being here in the woods but isn't it just a bit lonely?

They all three nod

> Then—how about it if you joined our circus?

They pause, look at each other, then after this silent quick discussion they nod heads like crazy

> Oh that's wonderful! That's great! And it's not work really, it's more like fun! Oh I know you'll enjoy yourselves! You'll meet all my friends and there's Mum and Ronnie and Joey and the acrobats and everyone! What do you say?

They jump up and down with great excitement

> You'll make a fabulous act! And I've just remembered something— (*with glee*)—you'll finish off Mr Bloodthirsty Black. He may have the biggest circus in the world but he's got no-one like you! We're in business! Circus business! SHOW business!

Music starts under her speech. She shakes hands with each of them as she sings

SONG 9

The Bears listen enthusiastically as she sings the lyric to them as though it continues the dialogue and then Goldilocks and the Bears do a very short and simple Routine

Black-out

SCENE 6

AN EVIL TELEPHONE CONVERSATION

The tabs close and in front of them Benjamin Black enters holding a telephone receiver with its cable reaching into the wings. A green spot covers him

Black (*into the telephone impatiently*) Hullo? Come on operator, come on! I want to get through to the gypsies who live on the common! . . . Ah . . . is that Campside oh-nine-two-four? I want to speak to Pedro, the Gypsy Chief . . . Is that you, Pedro? It's me, it's Bloodthirsty Black! How's the Caravan? . . . Good! *Been stealing any good things lately?* . . .

A couple of television sets and a tape recorder? Very nifty! (*He puts a hand over the telephone and addresses the audience*) He's almost as wicked as wot I am—only he's slimy with it. Ha ha ha! (*Into the receiver*) Pedro, me old mate, *I need your help*. I've just discovered that my rival Sadie Spangle has acquired a new act for her stoopid little Circus. It's called "Goldilocks and the Three Bears" and apparently it's sensational. The public is going to love them three bears—and that's bad news for Blood-thirsty Black. So, Pedro, me old duck. HOW CAN I GET RID OF THOSE THREE BEARS? (*He listens, warming to the evil plans he hears*)

The Lights start to fade

Yes . . . Yes . . . Oh, wicked, *wicked* . . . Oho . . . Oho . . . OHO . . . Yes . . . Right. (*To the audience, hand over telephone*) Listen, you lot. It's rude to boo when someone's talking on the phone—you haven't been brought up proper, so shut yer gobs! (*Into the telephone*) Great idea, Pedro! Thanks again! Ho, ho, ho . . .

A loud dramatic chord fades him out vocally, and the Lights fade to Black-out as he exits

Bright music. The tabs open

SCENE 7

IN THE CIRCUS RING

The same as SCENE 3(a), *but this routine is different in style. The Circus folk are already posed in Circus attitudes and one of them—either Sadie, Ronnie or Joey—starts the number*

SONG 10

A short routine for juveniles as toy soldiers could be included here

After the routine, all exit to applause and Joey the Clown bounces on, very excited

Joey How's yer father?
Audience All right!
Joey Lovely! (*He gives the thumbs up sign*) Ladies and Jellyspoons, there's a great big queue outside the circus tent! I'm sorry we've run out of seats, but we all know the reason! Ladies and Jellyspoons, presenting the act you've all come to see: GOLDILOCKS AND THE THREE BEARS!

Joey exits and Goldilocks enters in an attractive costume

Fanfare. She speaks over a percussion tempo

Goldie The drum goes boom
The trumpet blares!
It's Goldilocks
And her Three Bears!

She steps to the side of the stage and gestures

Father Bear!

Father Bear enters with a bowler hat, and a rolled umbrella which he treats as a walking-stick as he "soft shoe" dances to one chorus of soft shoe music. After a neat bow, he exits

There is taped as well as live applause

Mother Bear!

Mother Bear has a ballet skirt round her waist and a pretty hat or tiara on and she dances to some ballet music, and after a pretty curtsey, exits to taped applause

And now—Baby Bear!

Goldilocks exits. Baby Bear enters in American baseball cap and jazzy coat

He does a rock number, getting the audience to join in

At the end he does a big twist exit to the applause. Music continues so does the taped applause. Father returns for bow, ushers on Mother, both usher on Baby Bear who is twisting with Goldilocks now. They all bow over and over to the tumultuous taped applause

Black-out

SCENE 8

OUTSIDE THE BIG TOP

Tabs or Front Cloth, showing bright and garish outside of tent with a big advert for "The Three Bears" painted on the cloth

Benjamin Black enters furtively looking round. He wears a white overall and carries a peaked cap and wig in one hand, and in the other an ice-cream box with sling. He puts them on the ground as he speaks

Black Last night *this* Circus was full but d'you know how many were sitting in the seats of *my* Circus? Three adults and one Great Dane. (*To the audience*) Yes, the Three Bears are a great success, aren't they?

The audience make no reply, or a few "Yesses"

Aren't they!

Audience Yes!

Black Listen when I'm talking to you, you ignorant oafs! So the Three Bears are a big success—BUT NOT FOR LONG! Not when I've got Pedro the Gypsy to help me! (*He holds up clothes*) Here's a coat and cap the gypsies have just given me—they've stolen them from somewhere. (*He adjusts the overall*) And this wig is Pedro's idea as well! He said when I wear it nobody—not even Goldilocks—will recognize me! (*He puts it on*) You don't recognize me, do you?

Audience YES!

Black Oh shurrup. So, that's the coat, the cap and the wig. (*He puts on the peaked cap, like ice-cream salesmen wear*) Now we come to the best bit—*the box of ice-creams. (He puts the sling over his shoulders and "wears" the box, and starts arranging the ice-cream tubs*) In here are strawberry, vanilla, raspberry—oh, I've only got one raspberry one. (*He peers at the audience*) I can see some of you are eating ice-cream so will you do something for me. Will you give me a raspberry?

Audience: BBBRRRSSSS! Drop dead! etc.

Black (*enraged*) Not that sort of raspberry. (*Triumphantly*) But now you will see how clever my gypsy friend has been (*He holds up a tub*) HONEY-FLAVOURED ice-cream! Bears love honey, don't they, and in this tub is honey-flavoured ice-cream. But there's something else in this tub as well—SOME GYPSY POISON. Ha ha ha ha!

Goldilocks and the Three Bears enter. The Bears each pat their faces with coloured handkerchiefs, and Goldilocks fans her face with her hand

Black checks his laugh and assumes some character, such as a round-shouldered Cockney, and waits

Goldie Phoo! I'm hot after all that work aren't you?

The Bears nod

I'd love a cold drink or an ice-cream or something. Oh well . . .

Baby Bear nudges her

What's the matter?

He points to Black

An ice-cream man! What a strange coincidence! (*She laughs*) It's almost as though he was standing there waiting for us!

They move to Black

Goldie We'd like four ice-creams, please.

Black (*in some accent*) Certainly, my dear. (*He opens the lid and sorts out the ices*)

Goldie (*to the Bears*) Vanilla?

All shake their heads

Strawberry?

All shake their heads

Raspberry?

All shake their heads

Black What about—*honey* flavour?

All three nod their heads vigorously

Goldie Then I will as well. That's four honey ice-creams please.

Black Four honey ice-creams for Goldilocks and The Three Bears. That's forty p. each, my dear.

Goldie (*handing him the money*) There. (*She looks at him*) Haven't I seen you somewhere before?

Black I don't think so dear. I come from—(*local reference*)—and we don't see many people there.

Goldie I think I'll have . . .

Mother Bear taps her on the arm and whispers to her

"Never take sweets from a strange man!" Oh I know, Mother Bear, but he's just a nice old ice-cream seller. (*She is not sure, so addresses the audience*) He's just a nice old ice-cream seller, isn't he?

Audience No!

Black (*aside*) Silence! Shut yer traps!

Goldie No? But look at the dear old boy . . . He's WHO? (*Amazed*) He's Benjamin Black? (*She laughs*) Oh dear! (*To the Bears*) They say he's Benjamin Black! (*To the audience*) You do say some funny things!

The Three Bears laugh. Goldilocks hands out the tubs

One for you, Mother Bear, one for you, Father Bear, and one for . . . (*She takes the wrong one*)

Black No Miss—that's *yours*.

Goldie Oh, you want me to have this one and Baby Bear to have this one? But why? (*She does not give it to Baby Bear*)

Black Well, I think that one has got something else in it beside honey.

Goldie Oh lovely, has it? There you are then Baby Bear!

Black (*to Baby Bear*) It's especially for *you*.

Baby Bear is pleased and nods. They stand in a row with the tubs and scoop out the ice-cream with their paws, Goldilocks only uses a spoon. Pause. Simmering music. Pause again. Suddenly Baby Bear cries out and falls to the ground C. The others gather round him

Goldie What's the matter?

Goldilocks and Mother and Father Bear crouch by Baby Bear wondering what is wrong. Behind them Black pulls off his hat and wig, moving L as he does so

Black   Ha ha ha ha!
You thought the Bears would take away
The business from my show
But those that get in Mister Black's way
Live to regret it . . .

Belinda enters R

Belinda   NO!
You think you've won, but you've not my friend.
Goodness will triumph in the end!

Black You sounded like a Fairy
      When that funny rhyme was said
      But listen my little canary
      BABY BEAR IS DEAD.
      Ha ha ha ha!

Black exits L

Belinda is much concerned, and waves her wand at the wings

Sadie runs on, in a fantastic costume, with Ronnie and Joey

Joey How's yer father?
Audience All right!
Joey (*to the audience*) That wasn't very cheerful, what's up? (*He sees the group and realizes*) Oh . . .

Joey, Sadie and Ronnie gather round Baby Bear

Sadie What's wrong?
Goldie (*sobbing*) Baby Bear—look—he's been poisoned . . .
Ronnie Here, I saw a gypsy running away just then! (*He points to where Black went off*)
Sadie (*to the audience*) Was it a gypsy that ran away?
Audience No—BLACK, etc.
Sadie Black? Bloodthirsty Black? We must go after him!
Joey He mustn't get away!

Sadie and Joey start to exit

Goldie (*pathetically*) It's too late! Baby Bear's heart has almost stopped beating!

Sadie and Joey return, scared

Ronnie What shall we do?
Goldie Nothing we can do.

She turns to Ronnie sobbing, and he comforts her

Belinda You've all been kind to Baby Bear
       Unlike that horrid man—(*she points off*)
       So I must think of something
       That is, if I can.
       They say that somewhere in these woods
       Is a waterfall that's cool
       And that once—long, long ago—
       It was called "The *Magic* Pool".
Sadie (*surprised*) It's Pam Ayres.
Joey You mean in the woods near the circus?

Belinda nods, and, as seriously concerned for Baby Bear as the others, she continues

Belinda I cannot promise anything
       But just take Baby Bear

> Down to the nearby magic pool
> To drink some water there.

Ronnie That's right! I've heard it's a magic pool! (*To Goldilocks*) We can try . . .

Goldilocks nods

Sadie Bloodthirsty Black! You don't know what he'll do next! He's the Circus's answer to Enoch Powell! (*To all*) We'll give it a go—come on dears!

Joey and Ronnie pick up Baby Bear and start to exit, the others following

Goldie (*turning back to Belinda*) But whoever heard of a *real* magic pool? They only happen in fairy stories.

Belinda (*smiling mysteriously*) Do they?

> *Ronnie takes Goldilocks' hand and they follow the others, leaving Belinda alone*

The Lights start to change

> Mother Bear and Father Bear
> It's sad to see you grieve
> But miracles *do* happen
> To people that believe!
> Though Bloodthirsty Black may laugh at me
> And think that I'm a fool
> I'll summon the Fairy Guardians
> Of the Magic Pool!

Music

> *The Woodland People start to enter*

Belinda ushers them in, and the Dance Routine of the following scene starts. At once the tabs open, or the front cloth rises

SCENE 9

THE MAGIC POOL IN THE WOODS

Trees overhang a pool and the scene looks a bit unreal and silvery:-the trees are weeping willows. Painted on the backcloth, or using "silver slash" as water, we see the waterfall that falls into the pool that is behind the ground row of rocks and reeds and ferns. The waterfall is one side and a large rock is the other side and the wings are trees. The waterfall and the rock are the main features of telling the story

The scene opens with a short Dance Routine (No. 11)

> *After the Routine, a sad procession enters: Joey and Ronnie carry a litter with Baby Bear on it, followed by Mother Bear with a handkerchief to her*

eyes and Father Bear pats her shoulder in comfort, Sadie shaking her head in deep distress, and they all group round the litter. Goldilocks now enters and bursts into tears, and wipes her eyes

Belinda waves her wand, commanding one of the Woodland People to go up to the pool

Belinda You Guardians of the Pool attend!
　　　　See how they help each other
　　　　They're kind to all four legged friends
　　　　And treat them like a brother!

The Fairy Guardian seems to collect water from the lake upstage, brings down a half-closed flower as though it is full of water, and gives it to Sadie

　　　　Now let's see if my magic power
　　　　Will save the Baby's plight—
　　　　Give him the water from the flower . . .

Sadie puts the flower to Baby Bear's mouth. Pause. Baby stirs

Goldie Oh! He's going to be all right!
Sadie (*making a down-to-earth joke to break the mood*) What he needs now is some syrup of figs!

At this, the Group laugh and Baby Bear gets unsteadily off the litter, Mother and Father Bear kiss him, so does Goldilocks. Much joy from all, but Belinda warns them

Belinda Stay! Although your happiness I share
　　　　Of Bloodthirsty Black beware, beware!
　　　　Now you are all in this magic glade
　　　　More magic now comes to your aid!

Belinda waves her wand towards the big rock. There is a rumbling sound effect, a fanfare, and the Woodland Fairy People point to the rock. It slides back into the wings to reveal a lit grotto or alcove with a sword in it

　　　　That sword, Ronnie, you must take!
Ronnie *Eh?* But I'm just a bloke from the circus!

He is embarrassed and this makes Belinda impatient

Belinda It's name is Excalibur, the sword of the Lake!

Embarrassed, Ronnie takes it from the Fairy Guardian who has brought it to him

Ronnie I can't go waving this sword fore and aft!
Joey He's Ronnie the Ringmaster, it makes him look daft
Belinda You've *got* to beat Bloodthirsty Black
　　　　So you must do or die
　　　　Have confidence, have bravery!
　　　　Wave the sword on high!

Ronnie tries his best at a heroic stance, Goldilocks enthusiastically nodding encouragement, and he holds up the sword

Ronnie And so, my friends, we've got it made!
Joey Of course we have—it's a Wilkinson Blade!
Goldie Wave the sword and be brave as you can!
Sadie And, Benjamin Black—*you're a dirty old man!*

All cheer, wave the sword and their clenched fists in the air, and, at the end of a song (No. 12) place themselves for the Grand Tableau, as—

the CURTAIN *falls*

ACT II

Scene 1

THE GYPSY ENCAMPMENT NEAR THE CIRCUS

There are trees and caravans—the caravans can be cut-outs with practical doors and wooden steps up to them. A camp fire and a cauldron are set prominently. If the "Tree of Truth" routine is used, see Production Notes

OPENING NUMBER—SONG 13

Gypsy song and dance

Pedro Twoface, the gypsy leader, seems a breezy man and he gets the audience to clap in time to the gypsy song. After the number he chucks the girls under the chin and talks to the men, who salute their Chief

Pedro (*after the number*) Well, my friends, you've made the gypsy blood stir in my veins! Shall we dance it all over again?
All (*laughing*) No! Not again!
First Gypsy (*laughing*) Pedro will have his joke!

They all laugh

Ronnie enters. He is scared but then marches straight up to Pedro

Ronnie (*aggressively*) You, my man, are you Pedro the Gypsy Chief?
Pedro (*with much charm*) Yes I am, lad—welcome to our gypsy camp! And where are you from?

Ronnie moves to the fire and a smiling Girl moves to make room for him

Ronnie I'm the ringmaster of Sadie Spangle's Circus!
Pedro Sadie Spangle—oh, I know, isn't she the nice lady wot owns the Circus down the road?
Ronnie That's right!
Pedro I like you lad!

Pedro laughs heartily and slaps Ronnie on the back. Ronnie splutters and chokes

Well, now you're here what can we do for you?
Ronnie (*looking round*) I was told to look out for some wicked gypsies.
Pedro (*amused*) I don't think any of us look very wicked, matey!

All laugh

Ronnie (*laughing with them*) There must be another camp further down the road!

Pedro Yes there must! Er—who told you we were wicked?
Ronnie Sadie Spangle.
Pedro (*sinisterly, aside to the audience*) That's Goldilocks' mother, the old
bat. (*To Ronnie, cheerfully*) Have you, by any luck, come here *alone*?
Ronnie Oh no, Sadie and Joey the Clown are with me!
Pedro (*aside*) Curses. (*To him heartily*) Well bring them in, lad, bring
them in!
Ronnie Okay! (*He runs up stage, beckons*)

Joey enters, with a ridiculous Spanish gypsy hat and trousers

Joey (*calling to the audience*) How's yer father?
Audience All right!
Joey (*giving the thumbs up sign to them*) Lovely!

Sadie enters dressed like a full-blown Gypsy Princess

They do a quick bit of a mad dance, singing unaccompanied

*A gypsy Girl gives Sadie a big artificial rose and she puts it between clenched
teeth*

Sadie OW! (*She takes rose out of her mouth*).
Joey What's wrong?
Sadie It's a thorny problem. (*She takes an imaginary thorn from her lips*)
Pedro (*to Sadie*) Oh, my gypsy heart!
Sadie (*seeing him*) Oh, what a hunk of middle-aged man!
Ronnie We've come to the wrong camp. This friendly type is Pedro, chief
of the gypsies!
Sadie And I'm Queen of the May!
Pedro All those ribbons everywhere—you look like—like . . .
Joey Spaghetti Junction!
Sadie Thank you! (*She glares at him*)
Pedro Senorita, won't you come into my caravan?
Sadie Now steady on. Why should I?
Pedro You have the gypsy in your soul.
Sadie (*lifting up her foot and checking the bottom of her shoe*) Gypsy on my
sole? I think it's something else, but I may be wrong . . .
Pedro Viva!
All (*putting their hands up in salute*) Viva!

All exit except Sadie and Pedro

They go into the "Tree of Truth" routine sitting on a log

Pedro (*passionately*) Senorita, you're beautiful. Come into my caravan,
my little potted plant.
Sadie (*suspiciously*) You're always saying "Come into my caravan". What
d'you want me in your caravan for?
Pedro Er—no reason—(*obviously lying*)—just a cup of tea!

A large prop apple falls on his head from above

Ow! What's that? (*He rubs his head and looks upwards*)

Sadie (*pointing up*) *That* is a Tree of Truth. They're very useful for an innocent girl like me.

Pedro Why are they useful?

Sadie Every time a lecherous man like you tells a lie, a big apple bounces on his bonce.

Pedro Ridiculous. Anyway, I don't tell lies.

The second apple falls on him

Ow! Here, let's change places.

Sadie I don't mind . . .

They change places. Sadie sits in the place where Pedro sat, and Pedro looks upwards apprehensively, and sits where she sat

Now let's get this straight. I am a respectable widow so if there's to be any hanky panky, I want a marriage proposal first.

Pedro A marriage proposal? My dear senorita, I wouldn't even *touch* you until I had proposed marriage!

A third apple falls, this time from area (2)

OW!

Sadie That'll teach you to tell lies. I know your sort.

Pedro My sort?

Sadie Yes, your sort. You meet a frail defenceless young girl like me and just because you've got hot gypsy blood running through your veins like a Servowarm central-heating system, you think everything's for the taking.

Pedro I happen to think that you are beautiful. (*He looks up but nothing happens*) I happen to think that you are adorable. (*He looks up but nothing happens*) By the light of that camp fire, your face lit by its glorious glow, you look like Raquel Welch.

A fourth apple falls from area (2)

OW! (*He rubs his head and mutters furiously*)

Sadie Can't you ever tell the truth? I give you one more chance.

Pedro One more chance. Then why don't we get married? Come on, Sadie, give us a kiss.

Sadie Me, give you a kiss? Have you gone mad? Have you gone stark raving? Have you a screw loose? Why. *I've never kissed a man in my whole life!*

A mass of apples falls on her from area (1) and from everywhere else as well. Much noise from the percussion

OW! No! Help! No!

Sadie exits, yelling

Pedro remains, laughing. Dramatic chord

Black enters. It is clear he is scared of this gypsy place

Pedro stops laughing when he sees Black

Black (*calling*) Pedro?

Pedro is now evil and shifty

Pedro Oh, it's you. (*He spits*)

Black That gypsy poison didn't work.

Pedro Didn't work? What you talkin' about!

Black The Three Bears are well again. They're the star attraction of Sadie Spangle's Circus.

Pedro Stupid Sadie Spangle and stupid Ronnie the ringmaster was here not long since—the fools.

Black We're the fools. *That gypsy poison didn't* . . .

Pedro (*pointing at him threateningly*) Don't you speak to me like that. That poison *can't fail*. You must have mucked it up somehow.

Black (*shouting*) I tell you it didn't work!

Pedro (*shouting*) Don't you shout at me!

Black (*shouting very loudly now*) I'm not shouting!

Pedro You're always trying to *use* me! I'm fed up with Bloodthirsty Black and his bloodthirsty schemes!

Black But Pedro, old son . . .

Pedro Don't you old son me. (*Evilly*) We gypsies have magic powers, so be careful, my friend.

Black But Sadie's Circus is full every night and mine is *empty! I've got to get rid of the Three Bears.*

Pedro Who's stopping you?

Black (*whining*) They'll know I tried to poison the bears, so they'll try and poison *me*. It's not fair . . .

Pedro And Goldilocks is going to marry that Ronnie the ringmaster. *That's* not fair either.

Black (*giving a big reaction as he realizes*) You mean, *you fancy Goldilocks?*

Pedro Aye. We gypsies like blondes. My gypsy blood runs hot for her, fit to boil. That beautiful golden hair—she's a lovely little kid, she is . . .

Black (*to the audience*) Now I know how to get him—watch this. (*To Pedro*) I'll strike a bargain!

Pedro (*laughing, sarcastically*) What "bargain"?

Black If you help me get the Bears, I'll help you—

Pedro (*his sarcasm gone, eagerly*) Get Goldilocks?

Black I promise. Give me a drug to send Sadie to sleep, then I can grab the Bears . . .

Pedro And I can grab Goldilocks! Done! (*Calling*) Tino! Maria! Marco! Diddiccai!

Music

The Gypsies enter in twos and threes

The Lights fade down to a sinister, darkened stage

A powerful drug to make the flesh creep
To send even Sadie Spangle to sleep

By the dark of the moon, by the light of the sun
Zolleeta! Zolleeta! It shall be done!

He goes to the campfire. One of the gypsy Girls brings him a small coloured bottle, which he holds up. He speaks to it

Down Sadie Spangle's throat is your destination
Gypsies; help me with the incantation!

DANCE ROUTINE (No. 15)

Throbbing music, strange lighting, a sinister dance more voodoo style than the opening wild gypsy dance. Shadows on the backcloth, mystery. The cauldron lights up. During the dance, Pedro picks up a sack and throws nasty things from it into the cauldron, which steams

Legs of a rabbit, wing of a bat
All of a spider, tail of a cat,
Head of a frog, feet of a hen,
Toe of Anthony Wedgwood Benn,
Deadly nightshade wot I've found
Stir and stir and stir around!

The wicked dance ends with sudden freezing of everyone when Pedro shouts and there is a flash

(*shouting*) Eureka!

The dance ends. Applause, Pedro hands the bottle now full of the liquid from the cauldron—during the routine he has taken a ladle from the cauldron and ladled the vile concoction into the coloured bottle. Pedro hands the bottle to Black

This will take Sadie Spangle unawares!
Black Then you get Goldilocks—*and I get the Bears!*

They both laugh evilly, and as Black holds the bottle on high so all on stage scream out a gypsy shout

Gypsies Diddiccai!

Black-out

SCENE 2

GOLDILOCKS' DRESSING-ROOM

Tabs or Front cloth of a tent with a makeshift dressing-table and some costumes hanging up and a few circus tubs and props such as a papered hoop —all painted on the front cloth

The Lights come up on Belinda watching Goldilocks, who is in a fine party dress, straightening Baby Bear's big bow tie

Belinda Benjamin Black has some evil plan
            What it is, I don't yet know
            But I will help Goldilocks all I can
            And protect the Bears from that grotty man
            Wherever they may go!
            Unless I am very much mistook
            Trouble is just beginning
            Yet somehow or other, by hook or by crook,
            THIS FAIRY WILL SOON BE WINNING!

*Belinda exits with huge optimism on one side, as from the other side
Mother and Father Bear enter, she with a bow on her head, he with a white
collar and black bow tie*

Goldie Everybody ready for the party?

*Father and Mother nod, Baby Bear jumps up and down clapping, then does
some rock 'n' roll disco movements*

Sadie is giving it to say thanks to you three for making the Circus such
a success! Oh, Mum is ever so pleased!

Father Bear whispers in her ear, anxiously pushed forward by Mother Bear

(*Listening, then laughing*) You're worried about Bloodthirsty Black?
Oh Father Bear, we haven't heard of him for *ages!* He'll never trouble
us again! After all we're the success now and it's all due to . . .

*Goldilocks does a vaudeville "point" towards Baby Bear and shouts "Tararr!",
and Baby Bear clasps hands above head and jigs about with dance steps*

That's right! It's all due to—a dancing bear! (*She sings and dances with
them*)

SONG 16

*After her song and dance routine with the Three Bears, the Lights fade to a
Black-out and the tabs open or the front cloth is flown*

SCENE 3

SADIE'S PARTY UNDER THE BIG TOP

*The Circus Ring as in Scenes 3(A) and 7, but now with party decorations,
streamers, balloons, etc.*

*All the Circus folk, including Belinda, are chatting and drinking, the Gypsies
are now changed into party dresses or some may be in the circus clothes.
"Party music" is being played—a tinkling piano noise—and all are holding
glasses, Ronnie is chatting with them. Joey enters*

Joey How's yer father?
Audience All right.
Joey Lovely! (*He does a thumbs up to them*)

Goldilocks and the Three Bears enter and everyone applauds them

Ronnie (*announcing*) You all know why Sadie is giving this party. It's because our little Circus has become the most successful one in the country! So here is our hostess and our boss—Mrs Sadie Spangle!

Music. Sadie enters in an outlandish evening gown with a feather boa, etc.

Sadie Let everyone throw away their cares
Let everyone start drinking
To Goldilocks and the Three Bears!
(And I shall now get stinking)
And when I've flung a couple back
And got well and truly plastered
I'll drink a toast to Benjamin Black
The nasty mean old . . .
All *SADIE!*

Vamp music starts in vaudeville style, all get into position

Goldie (*toasting*) Let's drink to my Mum!
Ronnie Let's drink to Goldilocks!
Joey Let's drink to all beautiful girls, whoever they are!

SONG 17

Vaudeville introduction. Joey starts the routine, and to prevent it being static all six people move round as they sing the short chorus each time

	There was a young lady called Dolly
	Who went to a ball dressed as holly
Sadie	The prickly heat
	Soon affected her seat
Joey	When she sat down she said, "Oh my golly!"

All sing the short chorus

All	That was a beautiful name
	Give us another one do!
Goldie	There was a young lady called Mary
	Who fell in some cream in the dairy
Ronnie	A comical fellow
	Said "Cream is bright yellow"
Goldie	You look like a crazy canary!
All	That was a beautiful name
	Give us another one do!
Sadie	There was a young lady called Molly
	Down her throat there was stuck an iced lolly
Joey	When the doctor said "Cough"
	She thought he said "Laugh"!
Sadie	So that was young Molly's finolly.

All sing the quick chorus

First Girl There was a young lady called Beatie
Second Girl She slimmed in one day, very neatly
First Girl A number eight bus
            Without any fuss
Second Girl Came and flattened her figure completely.

All sing the quick chorus

Ronnie   A young lady named Polly Perkins
         Was ever so fond of small gherkins
Goldi   So one day at tea
         She ate forty-three
Joey   And pickled her internal workin's.

All sing the quick chorus

Sadie   There was a young lassie called Jenny
         As for money she just hadn't any
Joey   When she looked in her purse
         The problem got worse
Sadie   'Cos she wanted to now spend a penny.
All   That was a beautiful name
         Give us another one do.
Ronnie   There was a young lady called Nelly.

All stop the routine

Sadie Nelly? I'm not doing Nelly—it's full of traps, that name is.
Joey Oh go on—lots of things rhyme with Nelly.
Sadie Yes but they're all the wrong ones!
Ronnie Oh don't worry! Let's start again. (*He starts to sing again*)
         There was a young lady called Nelly
Goldie   Who ate far too much strawberry jelly.
Joey   Again and Again
         The poor girl had a pain
Sadie Well—er—(*triumphantly*)
         And the name of the doctor was Kelly.
All   That was a beautiful name
         Give us another one do.
First Girl A funny young maiden called Pauline
Joey   Had a face that was simply appalling!
Second Girl But she went to a hop
         And was top of the pops
First Girl With her twistin' and rockin' and rollin'

*All shout " Yeah!" and "Go for it Man!" and "Like there was no tomorrow!"
as all sing and dance a short rock number (No. 18)*

*Anything that will round off this routine jazzily, and maybe reprise Baby
Bear's Twist chorus. They do hand jive and some rock and jitterbug for about
sixteen bars. All yell "WOW!" to end the number with this twist reprise.
After it, all chat together noisily*

Carrying a glass, Benjamin Black enters

All react and gasp

Sadie (*furious at his cheek*) Bloodthirsty Black!!! What are you doing here, may I ask?

Black You're a success. I'm a success. Shall we let bygones be bygones?

Sadie Certainly not you constipated earwig!

Black (*with much false emotion*) I'm sorry for what I did. Really I am. Sorry. Ever so sorry.

Goldie D'you know, Mum, I think he means it!

Sadie Well—well as long as you don't offer me a honey ice-cream!

Black Oh no, I shan't be offering you *that*.

Sadie What does that mean?

Black I want to make peace not war.

Sadie Well—all right. It's a very nice idea.

Goldie (*now worried*) Mum—be careful.

Sadie signals that everyone should leave

All exit except Sadie and Black

Black Sadie, you look sumptuous! Why don't we kiss and make up.

Sadie You are awful, but I like you! (*She hits him hard*)

Black Why don't we become more than just friends . . .

Sadie He's full of Eastern promise.

Black You're a fine figure of a girl. You've got something the others haven't got.

Sadie Yes and what's more I'm clinging on to it.

He takes her hand and kisses it then travels up the arm

Black Eeny meeny miney mo.

Sadie (*slapping him*) That's as far as you can go.

Black (*looking round at the tent*) You and me understand about circuses. We're *fastidious*.

Sadie Yes I'm fast and you're hideous.

Black (*looking round*) I mean, you've got a beautiful big top.

Sadie (*draping her bosom a bit*) Cheeky devil.

Black I mean it's a beautiful Circus ring you've got here!

Sadie (*looking round at it, proudly*) I'm glad you like it! That's nice there isn't it—and that thing there! Yes it's got a bit of style!

She gazes round, and this is his chance: he takes the coloured bottle from his pocket and pours some of its contents into her glass

Black Well—bottoms up!

Sadie (*not drinking*) Yes it's a nice Circus . . .

Black I said bottoms up!

Sadie (*not drinking*) I heard you the first time.

Black Bottoms up. (*He holds up his glass in the action of drinking*)

Sadie You've got bottoms on the brain.

Black This is a good wine! (*He gestures her to drink*)

Sadie Mine isn't. Let's change over. (*She tries to change glasses*)

Black (*loudly*) NO!

Sadie What do you mean—"NO!"? (*To the audience*) Is he trying to make me drink this?

Audience Yes!

Sadie (*laughing*) You sure?

Audience Yes!

Sadie (*still laughing*) Never! Not after the ice-cream! Even Benjamin Black wouldn't try that one! All the same, thanks for trying to warn me and here's to you!

She raises her glass to the audience and drinks to them. Dramatic chord, then the music simmers

Black Ha ha!

Sadie What you mean, "Ha ha"? You are peculiar, Benjamin, sometimes and I can—(*she starts to slur her speech*)—never understand what you're up to—one minute you're—oh—nice and next—minute you're—ooooh —er . . .

The music is still simmering after the dramatic chord. She puts hand to her forehead. She starts to sway

Oh the boat's rocking. (*Calling*) Come in, Number Nine! Come in, Number Nine, time's up! (*Looking at him*) Benjamin, *keep still!* And why have you brought your twin brother with you? Oh what's the matter with me?

Black (*triumphantly*) You have been drugged!

Sadie What, like a hare?

Black I said, you have been drugged!

Sadie Oh I thought you said jugged!

Black Repeat after me: "You will obey my commands". (*He looks at her as though he is a hypnotist*)

Sadie (*as a chant*) You will obey my commands . . .

Black (*impatiently*) No, no!

Sadie No, no!

Black You will obey *my* commands!

Sadie You will obey *my* commands!

Black This is ridiculous.

Sadie This is ridiculous. (*All her replies with identical inflections to his*)

Black CALL FOR THE BEARS.

Sadie CALL FOR THE BEARS.

The Three Bears enter, Baby Bear in front

Black Ah, hullo, you three. *I'm Benjamin Black.*

Baby Bear runs round to the back and cowers behind Mother

Sadie was telling me she's sick of you three *and wants to get rid of you.* (*He points off*)

Sadie (*trance-like*) *Wants to get rid of you.* (*She points off*)

There is a terrible silence. The Bears cannot understand and look at each other. Father Bear puts out his paws in a pleading gesture

Black No!
Sadie No!

Mother Bear puts her paws out as a plea

Black No!
Sadie No!

Baby Bear puts his paws out

Black No!
Sadie (*after a confused pause*) No . . .
Black You're going to *another* circus so come on!

Baby Bear puts his paws to his eyes and starts to cry: but Sadie just stares out front with a blank zombie look

Sadie Oh I do feel funny . . .
Black (*to the Bears*) I'm taking you now to *my* Circus—The Black Circus.

SONG 19

The sad music to Sadie's song starts

Black exits, pushing out the Bears. Baby Bear turns and looks back at Sadie, pleading. Black returns and cuffs him, then pulls him off

Sadie is alone. The music continues

Sadie (*hand to head*) I don't feel very well. I've done something wrong but I don't know what it is—I feel I want to have a good old cry. (*As she breaks down, it starts to dawn on her what has happened*) What have I done? I've said good-bye to the Bears! I'm all confused—I'm so *unhappy* . . . (*She sings the short chorus of her sad song*)

At the end of the song Sadie slowly exits, weeping. Goldilocks enters from the opposite side

Goldie Mother? Mum? She must be in her tent, I'll talk to the Bears instead. (*She looks round*) I thought I saw them in here a second ago! (*To the audience*) Did you see them?
Audience Yes!
Goldie Where are they?
Audience Black—the bad man!, etc.
Goldie Benjamin Black's got them?
Audience Yes!
Goldie You mean Bloodthirsty Black has stolen my Three Bears?
Audience Yes!

Goldilocks continues asking which way, when did it happen, etc.

During this, Black creeps on behind her, ushers in Pedro, and points to Goldilocks. Pedro creeps down stage

Goldilocks is warned by the audience but she does not quite hear what they're saying. Pedro puts one hand over her mouth and other round her waist and drags her off kicking and muffled shouting

Goldie Help! Somebody help! Mum! Ronnie! Help!

Goldilocks exits, dragged off by Pedro and Black. Sadie enters

Sadie That's Goldilocks' voice! Something's wrong! I've just remembered something else—*I let Black take the Bears, didn't I?*
Audience Yes!
Sadie (*to the audience*) You let me do it! I hurt the Bears—I've never been so sad in my life—where are my Bears—who got rid of them? Who told Black he could have the bears? *Was* it me?
Audience Yes!
Sadie *Me?* Don't be ridiculous. Why would I ever let Bloodthirsty Black steal the lovely Bears . . .

Ronnie runs on

Ronnie What's up? (*To Sadie*) What's the matter?
Sadie (*hand to forehead, half recovering*) My head—I've been drugged!
Ronnie Drugged? What d'you mean drugged? (*He looks at her, shakes her, turns to the audience, with much panic and urgency*) *Has* Sadie been drugged?
Audience Yes!
Ronnie Who by?
Audience Black!
Ronnie I knew it! And where's Goldilocks? And where are the Bears?
Audience He took them, etc.

During the above all the Circus Folk, except Joey, enter and listen to the audience. There is terrible dismay. Panic music starts

Ronnie Goldilocks and the Three Bears have been kidnapped by Bloodthirsty Black!

The Circus Folk react with horror. Ronnie pats Sadie's hand

You go and lie down Gertie . . . the shock . . .
Sadie Yes.

Sadie nods and exits

Ronnie We must organize ourselves! We must find out where the Black Circus is! The Three Bears have gone—and so has my Goldilocks!

All sing a heroic song (No. 20) with Ronnie, at the end of which the Lights fade to a Black-out

SCENE 4

ON THE WAY TO THE BLACK CIRCUS

The scene is played in front of tabs or a front cloth

Pedro the gypsy drags on Goldilocks, who kicks and struggles

Pedro (*gloating*) Ha ha ha!
Goldie Let me go! (*She kicks him on the shin and thus stops his gloating*)
Pedro OW! They'll think I'm going to take you back to the gypsy camp but I'm not. I'm taking you to the Black Circus.
Goldie I don't care where you take me! It's my Three Bears I'm worried about, not me!
Pedro Don't worry about them. My mate Mister Black will soon get cracking.

Black enters with his whip

Black I'll get crackin' all right! Ha ha ha! (*He flicks the whip and cracks it*)
Goldie Don't hurt the Bears! Let me go! I want to help them!
Pedro Well *I* want my dinner. Come on, girl.

Pedro drags Goldilocks off, and they exit. The Three Bears enter, frightened of Black. They huddle in a forlorn group

Black (*to the audience*) Feeling sorry for the Bears are you? Want to collect some money to save the little dears? Want to have a *whip round?* Ha ha ha! Come on, you stupid animals. (*He whips at the Bears*)

The Three Bears scuttle across the stage and exit. Black waves his fist at the audience and exits to boos. Belinda enters from the opposite side

Belinda So that drug was made at the gypsy camp
That fact I did not know
As through the woods the villains tramp
Once again, I've been too slow.
I *promised* help to Goldilocks
But I've failed her day and night
Bless her little cotton socks
P'raps this will put things right.

Belinda waves her wand to the other side of stage and there is a trumpet call

Belinda exits as Joey enters, dressed as a Boy Scout

Joey How's yer father?
Audience All right!
Joey (*giving the thumbs up*) Lovely! (*He explains to the audience*) We've got to rescue Goldilocks and the Three Bears! (*He salutes with left hand*) Dab! Dab! We've got to attack the Black Circus! (*He salutes with right hand*) Dab! Dab! So I've called out the—(*local reference*)—Brownies! (*He salutes with both hands now and so drops his clip board*) Dab! Dab!

and Section, Section enter! Oh come on, Shirley Williams and Margaret
Thatcher! And you, Glenda Jackson and Barbara Cartland! (*He waves
to them to enter*)

*About four Singers (male or female) in ludicrous and badly fitting girl
guide uniforms with blacked-out teeth and pig-tails, shuffle in or march.
Some chew gum. Some have red noses and freckles and spots*

Joey Why are you late?
First Guide (*who is gawky*) We had trouble with our lanyards—didn't we,
girls?

They all giggle helplessly and bite their nails, etc.

Joey Pay attention and stand up proper. As we shall need proof of
bravery I will now display my medals.
First Guide (*pointing to a medal*) What's that one for?
Joey It's to hide a soup stain.
Second Guide Yes, but what is it?
Joey Heinz Tomato. Oh I see what you mean. I don't know. (*Proudly*)
But this one I won when we played darts against—(*local reference pub
team*)
Third Guide Where did you get that great big gold one?
Joey Woolworths. (*He points*) Oh yes, this was won on the frontier. (*He
turns around*) And this one was won on the backyere. (*He shows a big
medal hanging from his seat*)

*The four Guides laugh hilariously at the joke and then stamp their feet and
jump up and down*

Guides (*chanting*) Where is Say-dee? Where is Say-dee! Where is Say-dee?

Trumpet call

*Sadie enters as a Guide with a very large bosom indeed. Possibly it is two
balloons under a Brownie-style pullover. On her back are plenty of knap-
sacks, kettle, saucepan, etc., and maybe it all trails along the ground. She
holds a pole with a very small Union Jack on its end*

Joey Why are you late?
Sadie I'll be later still tomorrow.
Joey Why?
Sadie I'm not coming.
Joey (*pointing to the pole*) What's that for?
Sadie (*proudly*) It's Jubilee!
Joey Jubilee? That was years ago! What you talking about, Jubilee?
Sadie (*paralyzed with laughter*) Jubileeeve in Santa Claus!

*Sadie hands the pole off, or slides it off along the ground, while the other
Guides laugh in a giggly St. Trinians way and then play pat-a-cake*

Guides (*chanting*) Pat-a-cake, pat-a-cake, baker's man . . .
Joey (*as a command*) SHURRUP. Forward the Q.B.'s!

They line up by the side of Sadie

Oh blimey, what a shower you are! Close up

Sadie is not listening. He moves to her and speaks into her face

You Mrs Spangle, *close up.*

Sadie pulls her skirt up

No, not that way!
Sadie Oh, you mean *this* way? (*She turns round and pulls up skirt the other way*)
Joey Anyone else going to be difficult?
First Guide Scoutmaster.
Joey Yes?
First Guide I want to be excused.

All the other Girls gather round and hit her

Joey Back you fools, back!

They return to their places

So you want to be excused. What for?
First Guide (*coyly*) I can't tell you. (*She turns to other Guides*) Dare I tell him?
Guides Yes! Go on Mildred! Tell him dear!
First Guide Well—er—I've got a stone in my shoe.
Joey (*relieved*) Is that all? Then get into line. Stand to attention! Pull your stomachs in!

All do, and make loud sucking noises in air

Mrs Spangle, throw your chest out!
Sadie Right!

Sadie removes the padding from her bosom and throws it in the air. The Guides laugh helplessly

Joey Stop laughing! Listen to my word of command! You ready? (*He shouts*) Number!

A few bars of Latin-American music, and they all sway about

I said Number!
Sadie I thought you said Rhumba!
Joey No, no, *number.* (*Very fast*) One, two, three, four, five, six, seven, eight!
All (*very fast*) One, two, three, four, five, six, seven, eight!
Joey Slowly!
All (*very slowly indeed*) One—two—three—four—five—six ...
Joey (*in a desperate plea to them*) Please. PLEASE! We've got to get cracking! We've got to save Goldilocks and the Bears! We've got to get to the Black Circus! So *please*, get into line.

They do, and the Second Guide stands at the end of the line, near the wings

I want you to give me a nice final drill movement now. I want you to give me a right wheel!

The end Guide has reached into the wings for a toy bicycle wheel and holds it out

Second Guide Right wheel!
Joey Get rid of it!

The Second Guide hands it off

I want more discipline—*I* am giving the orders.
Sadie I'll have a Worthington.

They all call out their orders "large gin—double whisky—Coca-cola—meat, pie and chips, etc."

Joey We're marching off now! Come on—jump to it!

All jump in the air

Shake a leg there!

All shake their right leg

Right turn!

All turn right

We're off to the Black Circus now! (*As a command*) January, February *MARCH!*

All sing "Da, da, and the same to you" to the music of "Colonel Bogey", salute, march once round the front of the stage, and off

Black-out

SCENE 5

AT THE BLACK CIRCUS

Black cages are the main part of the scenery, the Lighting is dark—it is a sinister place. At an upstage corner is a sign "BOX OFFICE" and below is what seems to be a small window—where you pay for tickets—set into the wall or fence: but the sign and small window are in fact a secret panel that later slides back

Heavy music is heard. The Three Bears are on their knees, hunched together, shaking with fright. Black is pacing to and fro

Black (*gloating*) At last, the Three Bears are in my power! (*To them*) Now it's *my* turn to make you into a circus act—and I'm going to rehearse you 'till you drop! On the command "Hoop la" you will stand in a line and do the dance that *dear kind sweet* little Goldilocks taught you—the dance that gets the applause and the cheers! Right . . . on the command of hoop la, you will dance for Benjamin Black. (*He shouts*) Hoop la!

The Bears remain still. Black reacts with fury

Oho! So it's time for a sit down strike is it? (*Sneering*) I know what you're up to. You've heard that your stupid friends are going to try and rescue you. Well *I've* heard that as well. (*Bragging*) But your friends won't rescue you 'cos they won't *find* you! You three are going back right now into your *secret cage*! (*He laughs*) And no one will ever find you in your secret cage—not ever! Ha ha ha ha!

He runs up to the "BOX OFFICE" area, taps the scenery hard. Percussion effects. He stands back. The secret panel slides open, he whips the Three Bears inside, they are hidden from view, the panel closes again

(*Calling*) Guards!

Two Guards in black uniforms enter

You'd better patrol this part of the circus—I'm going to bed in my tent.

Black exits

Drum tattoo. The two Guards march across the stage, looking out front and all around, checking, then march back again

The Guards exit. From the other side, Sadie, Joey and Ronnie—with sword in belt—enter

Joey (*to the audience*) How's yer father?
Audience All right!
Joey (*giving the thumbs up sign*) Lovely!
Sadie So this is—(*local reference, preferably somewhere grotty!*)
Ronnie I'm glad I was given the magic sword—it looks as though I'm going to need it! I wonder where Goldilocks is?

Ronnie is about to cross the stage, but Sadie holds him back

Sadie Just a moment. Just a monument. I don't want you killed—have you read that? (*She points to a notice on the set*)
Joey (*laughing*) "Beware the Gorilla"—oh all circuses have that! It doesn't mean a thing!
Sadie You think so?
Ronnie It's just to scare off trespassers.
Sadie (*to the audience*) We don't think there is one, but if a gorilla appears will you let us know? Will you shout "gorilla"?
Audience Yes!
Ronnie Because we *must* find Goldilocks and the Three Bears!

Sadie, Ronnie and Joey gaze round

Sadie (*looking off*) Oh look, there are the circus kitchens . . .

The Gorilla stalks on, unseen

Audience Gorilla!
Sadie Yes that's right, there'll be a griller, there always is in a kitchen.
Ronnie I wonder where Benjamin Black kept those poisoned ice-creams?
Audience Gorilla!
Ronnie Yes that's right, vanilla! And strawberry and . . .
Audience Gorilla!
Sadie (*to the audience*) I do wish you'd stop saying "Gorilla". (*She reacts*)
   GORILLA?
Joey There's no gorilla! (*To the audience, laughing*) Is there?
Audience GORILLA!
Sadie Then let's look for it!

The Gorilla is now immediately behind them. They circle L with the Gorilla last in line so not seen by them. They circle R with same results—and the Gorilla is standing behind them as before: Joey—Ronnie—Sadie in line. The Gorilla taps Joey on the shoulder

Joey Yes Ronnie?
Ronnie What you mean, yes Ronnie?
Joey You touched me.
Ronnie I didn't.
Joey Well somebody did. (*He sees the Gorilla*) WAAAAH!

   Joey exits fast

Ronnie Joey's a funny bloke! He's just run away screaming because I
   talked to him!

The Gorilla taps Ronnie on the shoulder

   What's the matter?
Sadie Nothing's the matter.
Ronnie Then why did you hit me?
Sadie I didn't hit you.
Ronnie You did. (*He sees the Gorilla*) WAAAH!

   Ronnie exits

Sadie You know Ronnie, that Gorilla might have gone by now.

The Gorilla holds her hand

   You are nice, holding my hand to cheer me up.
Gorilla Ug, ug.
Sadie Pardon, indigestion, I need some Rennies. Oh what beautiful gloves
   you've got! Get them from—(*local store*)? They're quite like gorilla
   skin—(*unhappily repeating it*)—gorilla skin—oh . . . (*She sees him, then
   turns back to the audience*) Oh I quite like him! I like them big and
   strong you know. (*She smiles sexily at the Gorilla*) Hullo, cheeky!

The Gorilla screams and exits

   Charming! Oh well, no-one to worry about now! (*She sings to herself*)
   Tra la la la . . .

Pedro enters, then sees her

Sadie is terrified

Pedro (*sinisterly*) Well, if it isn't my little potted plant.
Sadie (*in a faint, hoarse whisper*) Ronnie. (*In a loud whisper*) Ronnie.
(*Speaking*) Ronnie! (*Shouting*) *Ronnie!* (*Yelling*) RONNIEEE!

*Yelling the place down, Sadie exits fast. Ronnie enters from elsewhere,
sword at the ready*

Ronnie Yes? Where are you, Sadie?
Pedro We meet again.

Ronnie looks round, sees Pedro, and gasps

Ronnie Pedro the gypsy!
Pedro Yes, Pedro the gypsy—and also, Pedro the *swordsman*. (*He takes his
sword from his belt*)
Ronnie My sword is magic—I'm not afraid of you!
Pedro Famous last words. Remember when you thought I was a *kind-
hearted* gypsy? I have two faces, haven't I?
Ronnie Then have at you, you two-faced twit!

DUEL

*Very loud duel music. Soon Ronnie succeeds in thrusting the sword under
Pedro's arm*

*Pedro gasps, drops his own sword, clutches at Ronnie's sword and exits
staggering, as though Ronnie's magic sword was through him*

Ronnie (*waving his arms*) I've won! Victory!

Sadie and Joey run in. Both now wear overcoats

Sadie Well done, Ronnie dear!
Joey Scotland for ever! (*He jumps up in the air, claps hands*)
Ronnie (*panting severely*) I'm—ah—ah—I'm exhausted—thank goodness
I won—oh—oh, I'm tired . . .

Black enters, also in an overcoat

Black Too tired to fight—*me?*
Ronnie (*horrified*) Fight you now? (*To Joey*) I can't fight him now, what'll
we do?
Joey (*scared stiff*) Well, don't look at me!
Sadie (*suddenly*) *I'll fight him!*
Black Madam, I was a professional wrestler.
Sadie That's all right! So was I!
Black YOU?
Sadie Yes! And watch out—I was known in the trade as Sadistic Sadie.
Black (*sniggering*) Sadistic? What's "sadistic"?
Sadie What I keep my knickers up with.

Black You floppy female, I'll soon finish you off. (*Calling*) Guards, bring on the wrestling ring!

Joey Bring on our lot as well! (*Calling off*) Come on, folks!

At once, we hear taped sound effects of the noisy crowd at a wrestling match waiting for the match to start

All the crowd from Sadie's Circus enter excitedly and become the cheering match spectators; already shouting. The two Guards from the Black Circus enter

Sadie's Circus crowd boos the two Guards on their entrance. One Guard has a square of canvas which he lays on the floor, the other has two posts with rope between them, which he puts downstage in front of the canvas square, to suggest a boxing ring. Joey takes off his overcoat and is wearing white shirt and black evening tie, maybe even dinner jacket. He is handed a practical hand microphone, or collects it from the wings. Black removes his overcoat to reveal a wrestler's dressing gown with "Bloodthirsty Black" on its back

Sadie (*calling*) You're just a bad joke!

Black (*calling*) Yes! I'm Bloodthirsty Black, the dirty crack!

Sadie removes her overcoat and reveals a wrestler's dressing gown with "Sadistic Sadie" on it

Sadie (*calling back*) And *I* am Sadistic Sadie, the tough old lady!

Black (*waving his arms about*) I've never lost a fight yet!

Sadie Except this one!

They move C and jig about impatiently, as Joey admonishes them both

Joey Now, do it fair. I want no rubbish. When the bell rings, in you go. Three falls or submit to my will. And may the best man—er—woman—win!

The Circus folk cheer as the opposing wrestlers get prepared

In the ring on the far side, weighing in at twelve stone six—Bloodthirsty Black.

We hear boos

And in the ring on this side—weighing in at fifteen stone eight . . .

Sadie Here! How did you find out?

Joey Sadistic Sadie . . .!

The taped crowd noises come up loud. We hear yells of encouragement and raucous advice, and the real shouts from Sadie's Circus folk

WRESTLING BOUT

Sadie and Black meet each other

Sadie (*to Black*) I'm a lady, so when I say start, start. And when I say stop, stop.

Black (*amazed*) What?
Sadie Start! (*She hits him and at once says*) Stop! (*She repeats this*) Start!
(*She hits him again and at once shouts*) Stop!
Black Just a minute! Just a minute!
Sadie Start—stop! Start—stop! Start—stop!
Black Ow—ow—ow—ow—ow!

*At this there is huge applause from the onlookers. Sadie does the arms
gesture of cutting the sound off—and at once there is silence. She then encourages the sound and we hear the crowd yelling full blast. She again cuts
the sound out, then encourages it again*

Joey Hey! This isn't right. Get into a proper clinch!

*Joey speaks a commentary into the microphone as they grapple for a while.
They clinch and Black trips up Sadie. They clinch and this time she trips him
up. They clinch, "ballroom dancing" music is heard, and they dance together,
realize what they are doing, and break away. Soon Sadie gets into her stride,
throwing Black everywhere until he crashes through the rope and is spark out.
There are grunts and groans from them both—Black "works" Sadie's throws,
making out she is flinging him about with huge muscular strength. Sadie wins.
Joey holds up her hand*

Joey The winner—Sadistic Sadie!

*Applause. Black lies on the floor in amongst the rope—indeed, he could have
been flung into the first row of the audience, if this is practical. He could find
Sadie's throw has flung him to the audience steps and he finds 'himself'
blundering down them, and he falls into somebody's lap. All cheer and praise
Sadie*

Goldilocks runs in

Goldie Oh Mum, you've won! (*She kisses her*) Ronnie, you *killed Pedro!*
(*She kisses him*) I escaped from the caravan!
Black (*on the floor*) You won but you'll never find the Three Bears. *Never!*
Ronnie (*threatening*) Where are they?
Sadie (*threatening*) Tell us!
Black Never! You'll never find them! You'll never find them! Ha ha ha!

*Calling "We'll find them—look over there—maybe they're in here"—they
search round the stage. The Circus folk chorus search each wing. The
audience shouts, the friends are thus guided to where the Bears are hidden*

During the audience participation, Black creeps away and exits unnoticed

*The friends feel round the scenery and, following the audience's advice,
arrive at the secret panel area*

Ronnie But it's the Box Office! It says so!
Audience There! That's it!, etc.
Sadie (*pointing at the words*) But it says Box Office!

*Ronnie finds the button and mimes that he is pressing it. The secret panel
slides back and the Three Bears come out*

Goldie (*to the audience*) Oh thank you for finding the Bears for us! Thank you. (*She brushes the Bears down and tidies them up*)

Sadie (*suddenly apprehensive*) Where's Bloodthirsty Black?

Ronnie I'll soon find him and when I do—well . . . (*To audience*) You tell me, what shall I do to him?

Audience Kill him!

Sadie You bloodthirsty shower!

Goldie Well, he's made so many people unhappy!

Sadie Wouldn't it be great if from now on he made everybody *happy!*

Ronnie and Goldilocks agree

Belinda enters

Belinda What you suggest shall now be done
              Benjamin Black it's time for fun!
              I'll use my magic on your behalf—
              Bloodthirsty Black—MAKE US LAUGH!

Vaudeville circus music as Belinda waves her wand towards the wings

Black enters in clown's hat and baggy coat with buttons. A red ping-pong ball plus elastic is on his nose

Black (*very vaudeville indeed*) I say, I say, I say! It's in all the evening papers! It's in all the evening papers! What's in all the evening papers? *Fish and chips!*

All (*groaning at the gag*) No, not that, oh blimey, no!

Belinda steps forward

Belinda Our story of two Circuses
              Is almost at an end
              Good circus and bad circus—
              From now on they shall blend.

Belinda waves her wand, there is a surge of romantic music. Sadie and Black move to each other

Sadie Benjamin!
Black Sadie!

Sadie romantically puts her arm in his

Belinda The Three Bears will be happy
              With all their circus friends
              And Goldilocks found Ronnie
              Was her hero, in the end!

At this, Ronnie puts his hands up in the air and shakes them above his head in the triumphant boxer style. Goldilocks laughs and kisses him. All cheer and Joey moves forward. The tabs close behind him

SCENE 6

BACK HOME

Tabs or front cloth as used before

Joey How's yer father?

Audience All right!

Joey (*giving the thumbs up sign*) Lovely! What d'you think of the show so far?

Audience Rubbish!

Joey (*laughing*) All right, then *you* can have a go now! I want you *all* to be members of the Circus, and we're going to sing a circus song—after I've murdered it! Right, I'll start. After three—SEVEN! (*He sings one verse and chorus of*)

SONG 21

Joey (*after it*) Now I think we need the trapeze artists to help us out. (*Calling off*) Tina, Mazeppa! Here they are, the Flying Hussars!

Two Girls enter in the acrobat costumes they have worn during the show, and hold between them the song sheet

Right, let's start. Ready? AND . . .

The audience sing a verse and chorus

Joey does not think the "Bom Boms" are loud enough so asks them to shout out "Bom! Bom!"

Joey And one more time!

At the end of the song Sadie enters in an outrageous—but easily changed—costume, a housecoat and a hat

Sadie That was terrible! Absolutely terrible!

Joey Well, if you think you're so clever, you can take that side.

Sadie All right. (*To her side of the audience*) So we'll show Joey where he gets off, won't we?

Audience Yes!

Sadie gets her half to sing. As they do so, Joey gets his half to boo them. Eventually all sing the chorus together

At the end of the song Sadie and Joey exit, waving

The tabs open, or the front cloth is flown

SCENE 7

Finale. The Wedding of Goldilocks—and Sadie

Music—reprise of Song 1 or Song 2

A glitter ball has been flown in to the set and is revolving and a spot is put on it. Perhaps one or even two trapeze bars are swinging from the flies with a girl on each

> *The cast enters in their circus costumes but with spangle cloaks over them, and take their final bows. Joey calls out his last "How's yer father?" when he takes his bow*

> *All cheer—as Ronnie and Goldie enter, they being the last to take their finale bows. She has a small white veil with white flowers for the headdress.*

The finale walk down and break into the finale couplets

Black The pantomime is over
         Alas, we've got to go
Goldie Good-bye now from Goldilocks
         Hope you liked the show!
Ronnie That's the end of our story
         There's nothing more to tell
Sadie But if you should ever meet Three Bears—
         May they bring *you* luck, as well!

FINALE CHORUS **(Song 22)**

During the chorus all throw paper streamers into the audience and balloons either come down from the flies or are hit on from the wings and into the audience—the Circus atmosphere is retained right to the end

After the final CURTAIN, *Joey pops out and yells "How's yer father"! Then waves a zany final good-bye*

APPENDIX

In ACT I, SCENE 2 *(page 12) Joey either calls into the offstage microphone or else pops his head through the tabs and calls*

Come to the Circus—come to the show!
Over to the Circus Ring—let's go!

SCENE 3(a)

IN THE CIRCUS RING

The Front cloth is flown or Tabs open to reveal the stage representing the Circus Ring, with the backcloth representing the rows of circus tent seats

Joey and Ronnie, plus all the Small Part Performers at the Circus are on stage. They have red ping-pong noses attached to faces by elastic round heads. Led by Joey and Ronnie, all sing

SONG 8

This can be just a production routine and end here. But it is far more fun for the cast and the audience if we develop the routine and show the Spangle Circus doing tricks. The scene should be played with great pace

After the short production routine, Joey and Ronnie remain, all others exit but the "Clown" music continues. Joey and Ronnie are each at a downstage corner and they alternately announce the tricks

Ronnie And now, folks, meet the Circus! As performed before all the crowned heads of Europe! Here is Willy Widemouth, the Sword Swallower!

Willy enters breezily to C and holds up a sword—A car aerial. He puts one end of it in his mouth and the illusion of "sword swallowing" works well as the aerial parts slide together, one inside the other. There is a chord, he bows and exits

Joey And here is Tryan! Yes, it's Tryan Liftit the Strong Man!

Tryan enters. He has put padding under his long sleeve vest, to represent biceps. He turns his back to the audience, "flexes his muscles", the music plays the cha-cha used on these occasions. Then there is a chord, he bows and exits

The remainder of the Tricks Routine is Ronnie and Joey alternately an-

nouncing the acts, or perhaps they also exit and the acts can enter in turn without announcement. The Clown music is played continuously and there are plenty of percussion effects and vaudeville chords to tag each trick. After the various tricks (see later), all enter and sing the final chorus of the Clown song and behind them the tabs close

When this final chorus is ended, all exit, the tabs open and reveal

SCENE 3(b)

As ACT I, page 13

So please choose whichever of the following fifteen tricks are suited to your cast and the running order I leave to you of course. Thus, SCENE 3(a) is simply a big comedy production number of circus tricks. It starts with a song, goes into all the TRICKS, and ends with the song again, this reprise being sung in tabs

THE TRICKS

Sadie (*in vaudeville style*) May I present—the Horn of Africa. (*She holds up an old motor-horn and hoots it*)

Joey enters

Joey Horn of Africa!? I thought you'd been buying sausages?
Sadie I have!
Joey I don't see any sausages—what did you buy?
Sadie A couple of Bangers!

At this, she holds up a pistol and fires upwards into the flies, down comes a string of prop sausages. They can be thrown on from the wings

As she and Joey exit one side Goldie announces

Goldie And here is—Tryan Liftit!

Two Clowns stagger on with a seemingly heavy barbell with weights at each end and they stand back. Tryan the weight lifter enters and makes much of taking talcum powder from the one Clown, powders his hands and gives back the powder. He then tries to lift the barbell, but in vain! The other Clown takes a large prop bar of chocolate with "Cadbury's Fruit and Nut" on it.

Clown (*calling*) Cadbury's Fruit and Nut! I thank you!

The Clown mimes giving some to Tryan who "eats it" and he then lifts the bar successfully. Triumphant chord. If preferred, cut the "Cadbury's" and have it that Tryan cannot lift the bar. Then a very young singer/dancer boy or girl enters and calmly picks up the bar and exits with it—followed by the other Two trying to cover up their confusion

Joey the clown and Mimi enter from the other side

Joey (*making the hand gestures*) Just like that! Just like that

Mimi What's that?

Joey Tommy Cooper! (*He kneels down*).

Mimi And what's that?

Joey Mini-Cooper. (*He lies flat on the floor*) I've been hit! I've been hit!

Mimi Who hit you?

Joey *Henry* Cooper!

They both exit, to vaudeville music

The trapeze artist lady enters with a plastic bucket and a Clown enters with two bits of rope. Several others enter with her

Iva I am Iva Sayftinette and here are two pieces of rope held by my friend. I put the two pieces of rope into the bucket, so. When we have said the magic word they will come out tied. One—two—three . . .

All ABRACADABRA!

She takes out of the bucket a large packet of "Tide" and all exit one side. Vaudeville music. At the same time the Sword Swallower enters wearing a very large prop glove, with the Lady Tight-rope Walker

She Why are you wearing *one* glove?

He Well it's in the weather report!

She What's in the weather report?

He It says it will be warm and sunny—*ON THE OTHER HAND* it might be cold and frosty! I thank you!

Both bow comically and exit

The other side Joey the clown runs in with a coloured hoop. He stands and shouts "Hoop la!" and rolls the hoop off into the R wing

We hear a sound effect such as a motor bike or sportscar and Joey "watches its unseen journey" right round the stage down to the L corner

Then another hoop—supposedly the same one—is rolled on from the L corner and he grabs it, shouts "Hoop la" and exits to a vaudeville chord of music

From the other side, a girl Clown enters with a circus tub or stool, places it down, and exits. "Heavy" music for the person about to enter in a gorilla skin and head mask

A boy or girl Clown enters with a Gorilla on a rope, and holding a whip. He whips the Gorilla who does not pay a blind bit of notice and soon sits calmly down on the tub and crosses his legs. The boy whips him again but he takes out a cigarette from the boy's pocket, and seems to light it with a lighter and have a couple of puffs. Finally, to a drum roll effect, he picks up the boy or girl and exits with them tucked under his arm

From the other side someone enters in a Chinese coolie hat, balancing several cardboard plates on something like a gas bracket/candelabra

Man or Girl (*in a Chinese accent*) I am a plate balancer from China and will now balance china plates. Ah—so.

After some business of carefully balancing, he or she bows and the plates are seen to be clearly stuck on to the gas bracket or whatever is used. He exits in confusion

From the other side, two Clowns enter and one holds up a toy dog, the other holds a hoop with paper stretched across it. There is a nylon wire attached to the dog's head and it's already threaded through a hole in the centre of the paper. The Clown holding the hoop is also holding the end of the nylon line

First Clown (*calling*) Ladies and gentlemen, Ponsonby, the performing poodle! He will now—at amazing expense—JUMP THROUGH THE HOOP!

Dramatic drum roll as the first Clown puts the toy dog on the floor with it facing the hoop. He moves a few feet from the dog and holds the hoop about two feet in the air. The second Clown now pulls the nylon line and that pulls the toy dog through the hoop. Cymbals clash

Both Clowns Viva! Olay!

They exit

Custard Pie

The other side a girl in a tutu enters and does a few classical ballet steps. Two Clowns enter each holding a cardboard plate of slosh and are laughing at her, pointing at her. They put down the plates of slosh on the circus tub and dance in comic imitation of her

They do not notice she has seen them and has become enraged. She balletically dances round the tub, balletically picks up the plates of slosh and balletically puts one in each Clown's face. All exit as the music plays a vaudeville chord

From other side a Clown enters and places a chair c. Flora enters and sits on the chair as Ronnie enters and announces

Ronnie Ladies and gentlemen, Flora Flingemmup will now sit in that chair and before your very eyes, she will vanish!

Another Clown brings on a coloured sheet and covers Flora. Two other Clowns cross with a five foot high hardboard screen or panel and stop with it directly in front of Flora. Drum roll. The two Clowns continue across the stage with the screen and exit. On the chair is the sheet with the person underneath

Cymbal clash—and now it is the juvenile boy or girl who jumps up, bows, and exits with the sheet and chair. In reality the juvenile had entered and Flora had made her exit by walking behind the screen as the Clowns brought it on and took it off

From the other side, Joey and another Clown enter. Joey carries a plank and the other Clown points to something. So Joey turns round and is thus about to hit the other Clown with the plank. But the Clown sees an imaginary flower on the floor and bends down and "plucks the flower", and thus misses the plank as it "sails" round

The plank is continuing its revolution and this time the Clown stands up and receives it at the back of the head—Boom from percussion. Joey laughs, so the Clown takes the plank from Joey and gooses him by putting the plank between Joey's legs. Joey stops laughing, yells and runs off, followed by the other Clown. Vaudeville chord of music

Two Clowns bring on a see-saw. A third brings on a chair and places it near the see-saw. Another brings on a second chair which he holds up in the air above him

Sadie enters and, as the music plays, she mimes to the audience that she will stand on this one end of the see-saw and Joey (or another) will jump off the first chair on to the other end of the see-saw. This will cause her—she mimes—to fly through the air and land on the second chair that the Clown is holding above his head. Sadie is now standing on the see-saw

There is a drum roll. Joey jumps on to the "up" end of the see-saw—and the see-saw breaks. Vaudeville chord and all exit

Two Girl Clowns or Majorettes enter holding a big decorated oblong panel, and unseen, someone has entered walking behind it. This person will work the illusion and remains hidden behind the panel

Joey and Sadie enter. He has a satchel over his shoulder. She stands in front of the oblong panel

Joey Ladies and gentlemen, I am standing in for Stanley Stiletto the knife thrower and that is my charming assistant Miss Sadie Spangle. I will now throw knives at her. I only hope I miss her!

Joey takes knife from satchel and mimes throwing it at panel. He does in fact put the knife back in the satchel quickly, after he has pretended to throw it

We hear a swannee whistle and what appears to be the handle of knife number (1) is pushed out from behind the oblong panel, through a slot that the audience cannot see

Joey now "collects knife number (2)" from his satchel but is in fact using the same knife and he again mimes throwing it at the oblong screen. Knife handle number (2) shoots out from the oblong panel from the second slot. All six knives are "thrown". The sixth is the tag

Sadie is all confident with big smiles. But the sixth knife handle comes out between her legs. She looks down, screams, takes—from where they are already tucked into her bloomers—a second pair of bright-coloured bloomers, and holds them up, horrified, as though the last knife has pierced the elastic of the bloomers she is wearing

Sadie *(as they bow)* How dare you! You might have ruined me for life!

How could you make such a mistake! Men! You're all the same!—wait till I get you back in the caravan, etc.

At this Sadie exits. The entire Circus Troupe apart from her enters with plastic buckets, singing the final chorus the Clown song. They line the footlights and as soon as possible tabs close behind them

At the coda of the song, they hold back the buckets as though about to hurl out the contents

All One—two—three—GO!

They throw out the contents, which luckily are merely torn up bits of paper. They go all over the band, footlights, or even the front row of audience. All exit singing a vaudeville-style coda

The tabs now open to reveal—

SCENE 3(b)

INTERIOR OF SADIE'S TENT

FURNITURE AND PROPERTY LIST

ACT I

SCENE 1

On stage: Circus tent (part seen) with flags, ropes, etc.

Off stage: Large flower (Circus Performer)
Pile of wrapped presents (Circus Performers)
Wrapped pound of coffee (Ronnie)
Newspaper (Ronnie)
TV set cut-out (Circus Performers)
Squeegee bottle, 2 "kinky boots", 3 tins of fruit, packet of porridge
oats, 5 bra's, packet of fish fingers, other props as desired (set
behind TV cut-out)

Personal: **Joey:** large trick handkerchief, tin of vegetables, comedy "blower"
Sadie: handbag with chocolate biscuits

SCENE 2

Personal: **Black:** bull whip, 3 £1 notes
Belinda: "wings", wand

SCENE 3 (a)

Circus Production Routine: for props used in this variable sequence
see text, p. 53

SCENE 3 (b)

On stage: Small bed or mattress with cover
2 small tables, crates or shelves. *On them:* pile of bills
Carrier bag. *In it:* sliced loaf, jar of honey

Off stage: Pound notes (Goldilocks)

SCENE 4

Off stage: 3 police helmets (3 Bears)

SCENE 5

On stage: 3 chairs in graduated sizes
Table. *On it:* 3 porridge bowls in graduated sizes, 3 spoons
3 beds in graduated sizes
Cupboard. *In it:* carrier bag

SCENE 6

Off stage: Telephone and cable **(Black)**

SCENE 7

Personal: **Father Bear:** bowler hat, rolled umbrella
Mother Bear: hat or tiara, ballet skirt
Baby Bear: baseball cap, jazzy coat

SCENE 8

Off stage: Ice-cream box with sling **(Black)**

Personal: **Black:** white overall, peaked cap, wig
3 Bears: coloured handkerchiefs
Goldilocks: coins

SCENE 9

On stage: Trees, ground row of rocks, reeds, ferns
Waterfall effect
Half-closed flower
Grotto behind sliding rock. *In it:* sword

Off stage: Litter **(Joey, Ronnie)**

ACT II

SCENE 1

On stage: Trees, cut-out caravans with practical doors and steps
Camp fire
Cauldron and ladle
Bench or log
Apples (rubber balls), for Tree of Truth routine (see Production Notes)
Sack of items for cauldron

Off stage: Large artificial rose **(Gypsy Girl)**
Small coloured bottle **(Gypsy Girl)**

SCENE 2

Personal: **Baby Bear:** big bow
Mother Bear: big bow
Father Bear: white collar, black bow tie

SCENE 3

On stage: Party decorations, streamers, balloons, etc.

Off stage: Full glasses **(Circus Performers)**
Full glass **(Black)**
Full coloured bottle, from Scene 1 **(Black)**

SCENE 4

Off stage: Clip board **(Joey)**
Knapsack, kettle, saucepan, pole with Union Jack **(Sadie)**
Toy bicycle wheel **(Girl Guide)**

Personal: **Girl Guides:** chewing gum
Joey: medals
Sadie: 2 balloons

SCENE 5

On stage: Black cages
Secret panel in fence or wall, with BOX OFFICE sign and apparent small window
Black stool
Sign—BEWARE THE GORILLA

Off stage: Square of canvas, 2 posts with rope **(Guards)**
Practical hand microphone **(Joey)**

Personal: **Pedro:** sword in belt
Black: "ping-pong ball" nose, with clown costume

SCENE 6

Off stage: Song sheet **(Acrobat Girls)**

SCENE 7

On stage: Glitter ball
Trapeze bars (optional)

Off stage: Balloons, paper streamers **(Cast and Stage Management)**

LIGHTING PLOT

Property fittings required: camp fire, cauldron fire
Various settings on open stage and front cloth

ACT I
To open: Full exterior lighting

ACT II
To open: General exterior lighting, camp fire lit

EFFECTS PLOT

ACT I

Cue 1   **Goldilocks** leans back in the chair   (Page 18)
Splintering effect

Cue 2   At end of each performance during **Goldilocks** and **3 Bears**
       act   (Page 22)
Taped applause

Cue 3   **Belinda** waves wand towards rock   (Page 27)
Rumbling effect

ACT II

Cue 4   **Pedro** throws items into cauldron   (Page 33)
Steam effect from cauldron

Cue 5   **Joey:** "Come on, folks!"   (Page 48)
*Taped noisy crowd sounds: continue throughout wrestling
bout, with momentary silences when* **Sadie** *cuts off applause
with gesture*

MADE AND PRINTED IN GREAT BRITAIN BY
LATIMER TREND & COMPANY LTD PLYMOUTH

MADE IN ENGLAND

Milton Keynes UK
Ingram Content Group UK Ltd.
UKHW052344150923
428750UK00034B/238